CREATING A
THRIVING
BUSINESS

"I can highly recommend this book to anyone starting a business, or who wants to spur their business growth. *Creating a Thriving Business* shows you how to systematically eliminate the guesswork and uncertainty associated with trying to grow a business."

—Bob Bare
author of *More Power! An Entrepreneur's Roadmap to Success*
founder of Best Selling Experts

"George Horrigan is obviously an author you can trust. He gently takes you by the hand and leads you to success as a business owner. He does not make it sound easy. But he does make it sound possible. He does not regale you with tales of how quickly it will happen. But he proves to you that it will happen eventually. Even God had to wait. For you, as for Him, it will be worth the wait."

—Jay Conrad Levinson
Author of the *Guerrilla Marketing* series

CREATING A
THRIVING
BUSINESS

*How to build an immensely
profitable business
in 7 easy steps*

GEORGE HORRIGAN

NEW YORK

CREATING A THRIVING BUSINESS
How to build an immensely profitable business in 7 easy steps

ISBN 978-1-61448-346-5 paperback
ISBN 978-1-61448-347-2 eBook
Library of Congress Control Number: 2012944095

Morgan James Publishing
The Entrepreneurial Publisher
5 Penn Plaza, 23rd Floor,
New York City, New York 10001
(212) 655-5470 office • (516) 908-4496 fax
www.MorganJamesPublishing.com

Cover Design by:
Rachel Lopez
www.r2cdesign.com

Interior Design by:
Bonnie Bushman
bonnie@caboodlegraphics.com

In an effort to support local communities, raise awareness and funds, Morgan James Publishing donates a percentage of all book sales for the life of each book to Habitat for Humanity Peninsula and Greater Williamsburg.

Get involved today, visit
www.MorganJamesBuilds.com.

To the God of the Universe
who desires us to thrive in Him

TABLE OF CONTENTS

Chapter Summaries

CHAPTER ONE

Taking time to choose the right business for you is critical to your venture's success. This chapter looks at the key factors involved in deciding what business you should start, including considerations such as location, financing, and timing, which you need to address before opening your doors. The chapter ends with tips on avoiding the "tyranny of the urgent" and dealing with the inevitable business "chicken-and-egg" syndrome.

CHAPTER TWO

Whether you have an existing business or are starting a new one, the ultimate goal is to have a *thriving* business. This chapter outlines the building blocks of a successful business, where things tend to go wrong, and how the Structure of Profitability™, whose seven steps are detailed in the remaining chapters, leads you to the business you want.

CHAPTER THREE

Vision is the first of the seven steps to creating a thriving business. Vision identifies the direction in which you want to take your business, its "destination" and what success for your business looks like. In this chapter, you will learn why Vision is so important, how to develop a compelling Vision for your business, and how to use that Vision to guide your business to success.

CHAPTER FOUR

Step two is identifying your Critical Success Factors, which are the things your business *must* do to achieve the Vision for your business. As opposed to the traditional daunting business "strategic plan," determining your Critical Success Factors allows you to craft a workable, actionable plan that can be executed one step at a time. Learn how to identify your Critical Success Factors in each of the key business areas of your business and deploy your business's limited resources where they have the most impact.

CHAPTER FIVE

The third of the seven steps within the Structure of Profitability™ is Marketing. You can have the best business idea in the world but if no one knows about your product or service, your business won't thrive. This is Marketing. First you will see how to determine who is your customer—your target market. Then you learn the secrets of developing and marketing a product or service that is astonishingly attractive to your customer. Next you will learn how to promote your product or service to that market. Also here are the steps you need to take to stand out from your competitors.

CHAPTER SIX

Through your Marketing area, step three, you determined who are your customers and what need you fulfill for them. You have developed the attractiveness of your solution to those customers' needs and you have made them aware of your product or service. Because Marketing only plants the seed, this chapter covers the fourth step, Sales or closing the sale, which harvests the fruit planted and watered in great Marketing. Determining optimum delivery channels, effective sales processes, and how to get beyond the "walled city" of your customer are all revealed in this chapter.

CHAPTER SEVEN

Whether your business is a restaurant or an industrial manufacturer, you have a "production area." This fifth step is where your business executes the game plan set forth so far to effectively and efficiently produce revenue.

Cost, quality, convenience, customer service, and the uniqueness of your product all come into play. This chapter covers all these key ingredients of the Production formula.

CHAPTER EIGHT

The sixth step, the Financing of Your Business is often one of the core areas of business least understood by business owners and leaders. This chapter takes the mystery and trepidation out of this key factor in creating a profitable business. From start-up needs to ongoing operational expenses to financing an expansion, this chapter not only breaks it all down for you but also covers sources of each kind of financing.

CHAPTER NINE

Through innovation and systematization, working *on* your business rather than *in* your business, the seventh step is critical to business success and satisfaction over the long term. In order to make this shift, you need an execution strategy for Innovating and Systematizing your business. This is how your business will grow, become immensely profitable, allow you to work fewer hours for more profit, and ultimately pass your business to your children or sell it for a profit. This chapter explains it all.

Acknowledgements

I would like to thank Jerry L. Little of CEO Support Systems for his foundational work in the business planning arena.

INTRODUCTION

If you are reading this book, then it is obvious that you want to have a thriving business, which means either you already have or want to start a business. You're in good company—various studies have shown that around 80% of people would like to have their own business! However, the vast majority of this 80% of people do not own a business. Why is that?

The data from the 2010 census shows about 30 million businesses exist in the United States. With an adult population of about 235 million people in 2010, the actual ownership of businesses in America is about 13%.

Why is the percentage so low of actual business owners compared to those who want to have their own business? They are overwhelmed by the thought of having a business, and they do not really know where to start. I have seen this first hand in my work over the past few years with several large university-based business incubators.

With regard to being a business owner, people tend to fall into one of four categories:

1. People who have a dream about owning a business but never act on their dream.

2. People who act on their dream to own a business but never get the business off the ground because they never get around to focusing on the business. Generally this takes the form of mentally deciding to start their business, but physically doing little or nothing at all to begin operations.

3. People who do start a business but lack the business knowledge, skill set, time, drive, determination, etc. that it takes to grow the business; therefore, it stays a small, part-time business, almost more like a hobby.
4. People who properly apply themselves and their skill sets to their business with the result of an operating business.

This book is aimed at people in all four of these categories. For those who fall into the first three groups, it provides a systematic way to start and grow a business. For people in the fourth group, the book will greatly shorten the time and effort involved in taking their business from wherever it is currently to becoming a strong and thriving business.

The methodology that I will share with you eliminates the trial-and-error, guess work, uncertainty, the "what to do next" and the "leap of faith" that plague so many business owners. The goal is to eliminate the situation that I see too often, where the challenge of creating a thriving business is so overwhelming that a person gets stuck somewhere on the road to achieving the hopes and dreams for their business.

If you are a business owner or you want to be one, this book is perfect for you. It lays out a logical, easy-to-understand, step-by-step blueprint in developing a thriving and successful business. The objective is that not to just start a business and then see it languish—you want to ensure that you have a phenomenally successful business!

Having worked with over 1,200 business owners in the past 17 years and having started seven businesses personally, I have learned what it takes to be successful with a business. So whether you are getting ready to start a business or if you have already started your business, the concepts that I present are indispensable in ensuring that you have the best chance of creating a thriving business. I developed this methodology and use it in all my businesses on a minute-by-minute, hour-by-hour, and day-by-day basis because it works—and it will work for you too!

The material covered in *Creating a Thriving Business* will ensure that you have the tools to enable your business to become all that it possibly can be. Many books have been written that spell out in a checklist fashion the activities that you need to engage in to start a business. These activities do not ensure that you will have a *thriving* business, only that you will start a business. These books identify the "nitty gritty" things to start a business but they may miss the big picture of what produces a truly thriving and successful business. The nitty-gritty approach results in a business owner being so focused on the "trees" of a business that they miss the overall foundation of why the "forest" (your business) was planted in the first place. This book covers the big-picture issues as well as the nitty-gritty and how they relate to each other.

If your business is already up and running, then the methodology introduced here will guide you in making sure your business is going in the right direction. Even if your business is already operating, I suggest you still read Chapter 1—Choosing a Business. You will gain some insights into your business and its future potential—knowledge that may lead you to make some changes to the very character of your business. The strategies covered throughout this book will enable you to examine the foundation of your business and determine if you want to change the overall direction of your business or its business model. If you have an existing business, the methodology that will be presented applies to you and your business whether you have:

1. A business that is just a few years old and is still in the start-up phase.
2. A small business that has been operating for many years but it has not yet flourished or taken off.
3. An older and/or larger business you feel has not reached its full potential or is not operating the way it should.

There are seven steps to creating a thriving and successful business. Chapter 2 provides an overview of the seven steps, and the seven actual steps begin with Chapter 3 and continue through Chapter 9. Listed below is an outline of how the following chapters will fit together in putting the "meat on the bones" of creating a thriving business.

1. Choosing a Business
2. Recipe for a Thriving Business
3. Step # 1—Vision
4. Step # 2—Critical Success Factors and Strategy
5. Step # 3—Marketing
6. Step # 4—Sales and Related Areas
7. Step # 5—Producing Your Product or Service
8. Step # 6—Financing Your Business
9. Step # 7—Execution—Innovating and Systematizing

I would like to say one last thing to the business owner who is thoroughly discouraged with their business and who is about to throw in the towel and give up: There is always hope for a business. Having started two unsuccessful businesses in the 1980s and having faced various challenges in five subsequent successful businesses, I want you to know that I understand and feel your disappointment and discouragement that your business has not turned out like you dreamed it would. But I have great news for you. If you absorb and implement the concepts discussed in this book, you *can* turn your business around.

To give you some real-world examples from people I have worked with, I've started each chapter with a "challenge" that real business owners have faced. At the end of the chapter is the "solution" we came up with together. Although the names and some details of the situations have been changed to protect my clients' privacy, these are drawn on real cases I have worked with. I hope they provide you with some of that old "misery loves company" and in the end with some inspiration that business challenges can be successfully faced head on and overcome using the methodology I outline in this book.

With that said, let's get started on creating a thriving business!

ᘔᘔ

THE WORKBOOK

Creating a Thriving Business has a companion workbook that will be invaluable for getting your arms around the strategic issues in your business as well as executing its detailed tasks. Available in electronic format at *www.FountainheadConsultingGroup.com*, and found under *Resources, Products* and then *Workbooks*, you can purchase this separately and follow along with the workbook tasks throughout each chapter.

ᘔᘔᘔ

CHOOSING A BUSINESS

ƨƨƨ

THE CHALLENGE

Greg was a tall, thin retired engineer who had grown restless in his retirement and was looking for something to do. He was an energetic, analytical person who was also very people-oriented. Greg had been very successful in his previous career as a sales engineer. As he pondered his situation, he realized that starting a business would be a very good use of the extra time that he had on his hands. I challenged him to think about the following questions: What kind of business should I start? What do I actually want to do with my life? What am I good at? What do I really like to do? Can I make a living at it? Besides making money, can I do something that would make the world a better place? What customer should I serve? What product would I provide to them? Do I have enough money to start this business? Am I temperamentally suited to start and operate a business?

ƨƨƨ

The very first step in creating a thriving business is to decide what business to operate. But how do you choose what business to start? What should motivate you to choose a particular business?

I am often asked, "What businesses are most profitable?" or "In what industries are people the most successful?" I have seen clients with thriving businesses in virtually any industry. Having a flourishing business comes down to three factors:

1. Choosing the correct business for you
2. Choosing the best model for your business
3. Running your business well

This chapter covers choosing the correct business for you. The next eight chapters cover how to develop your business model so that you run your business optimally, resulting in a thriving business.

If you already have a business, I suggest you still read this chapter. In my experience working with several business incubators, I have found that the first, second, or even third business that people start often ends up not being the business that they originally envisioned. Consequently they end up changing businesses, or changing the focus of their current business. Therefore, the topics that we will discuss in this chapter may be very applicable to you even if you already have a business.

First, let's talk about the three main ways to choose what business you are going to start.

LOOKING INSIDE: IDEAS FROM WITHIN

The traditional way of choosing a business has been to look inside of yourself, understanding yourself to "discover" a specific business that would be right for you. The outcome from this step may be a specific business or indication of a general direction about what kind of business may be appropriate for you. This approach is a very established way to determine which business would be right for you. But what does "looking inside yourself" really mean? Here are five basic questions to explore:

1. What are your dreams?
2. What is your life purpose?
3. What do you enjoy doing?
4. What do you do better than most other people?
5. Can you earn a decent living at it?

1. What are your dreams?

What are your dreams for your life? These could be new dreams or dreams from the past. As you reflect on these dreams, wishes, and goals, envision how they could translate into a business. Do not discard any idea as impractical or "wacky." Write down your dreams so you can go back and mull them over.

Complete exercise 1-1 in workbook

2. What is your life purpose?

To discover your life purpose, ask yourself questions like:

- What things am I passionate about?
- What things are important to me?
- What things get me excited and energized?
- Is there something that I feel I just have to do to help society or mankind?

As you consider the above questions, imagine if any of these passions could become the foundation for a business. Write these down and, once again, do not discard any idea or thought as infeasible or unrealistic. What may assist you with this step is to create a "personal purpose statement" and consider that statement in light of a possible business.

Complete exercise 1-2 in workbook

3. What do you enjoy doing?

As you take the time to review and examine all aspects of your life, think about what you really like to do. How do you spend your spare time? What do you enjoy doing and would do even if you were not getting paid to do it? Keep in mind that there are degrees of enjoyment; that is, do you *like* doing something versus do you *love* doing something? Try to find things or activities that you love. Consider activities that you do in your spare time or things that you just do for "fun." Make a list.

Next, make a list of unique experiences or accomplishments whose process you greatly enjoyed. A tool that may help is to write down your personal life history from your childhood until now including the unique experiences that have shaped and molded the person you are today. By writing down your life history and your unique life experiences, you may be able to discover an idea that could translate into a business.

This step is actually more important than many people realize—a number of studies have shown that if you do something you really enjoy, you will do it better than others, and you will be much more successful than a typical person in the same profession. Whereas, if you just go into a job only for the pay or start a particular business just because you think it would be a profitable business, but you do not really *like* the business, either you will not be successful or as profitable than if you greatly enjoyed the very nature of the business.

Complete exercise 1-3 in workbook

4. What do you do better than most other people?

We each have a unique set of aptitudes, skills, and abilities. When you play to your distinctive strengths, you will be more successful than if you ignore or play against your strengths. To understand your unique gifts and strengths, you need to ask yourself:

- What do I do better than most other people?
- What things come easy to me but are hard for others?
- Are there certain occupations or businesses that people have told me that they thought I would be good at?
- Are there certain businesses that I feel I would be great at?

If the bulleted questions above do lead you to a possible business, you also need to contemplate, "Does this particular business use my current skill set or training or do I need to get a new skill set, obtain additional training or education or develop new expertise?"

Also consider that even if you have a certain skill set, background or degree, if you do not like or enjoy the activity or you are no longer interested in this area, you do not want to pursue a business in an area just because you can do it better than most other people. Related to this issue is the situation some people find themselves in where they are just "burned out" or no longer have the drive or zeal for a certain area, even though they have training or are very good at it. As we discussed above, you will be more successful at something and enjoy your business more if you do something that you totally take pleasure in; if you do not care for liver, life is too short to eat it every day just because it is healthy for you.

Complete exercise 1-4 in workbook

5. Can you earn a decent living at it?

The first four questions will give you a large number of possible businesses. Cull this list down to only the businesses that are economically viable. Generally people or other businesses will not pay for something that is relatively simple that they can do themselves or something that can be accomplished fairly quickly.

DEFINITION: PRODUCT

I use the term "product" as a generic term that includes activities, services, or products that a business could produce; in reality, whatever your business produces, it is your "product."

Then what?

You now have your list of business ideas. There are three basic criteria you should use to evaluate each one:

1. Does this product require a unique skill set that only certain people (you being one) possess? This means that some aspect of your product is fairly complex and requires know how that is not easily obtained.
2. Is this a burdensome, time-consuming activity or product that people are willing to pay someone else to relieve them of?
3. Is this product or the outcome from it important enough to your target audience that they are willing and able to hand over their hard-earned money to you? Generally people are inclined to pay for products that are related to their:

    • Business
    • Enjoyment of life
    • Entertainment
    • Family well being
    • Finances
    • Happiness
    • Health
    • Personal fulfillment

There also must be a sufficient number of target customers for your product.

A telltale sign of a desirable product is if people are going to school to learn a skill in order to deliver your product. Another indication of the desirability of your product is if the market for it is growing quite briskly. Keep in mind that it is easier to succeed in a fast-growth market that has large market potential; in these types of industries most businesses have somewhat of an equal footing. And the growth in the market tends make up for mistakes that the owner may make.

Complete exercise 1-5 in workbook

LOOKING OUTWARD: IDEAS FROM THE WORLD AROUND YOU

A second approach for choosing a business is to look *outside* yourself for a potential business. Instead of examining who you are, what you like to do, and what your current skill set is, this technique involves looking for a problem that needs to be solved. This involves two basic steps:

1. Look at every problem you encounter during the day as a possible business or an invention that could lead to a business.
2. Ask yourself: in an ideal world, how would this need be met or fulfilled?

Every problem is a possible business

From the moment you wake up to the time you go to bed, consider anything that does not go 100% smoothly during the day as a possible business or an invention that could lead to a business. You will begin to look at your day and the world in a totally different way. Whenever you encounter a "problem," ask yourself, what would be a great solution to this problem? What will happen is that you will no longer see these things as problems, shortcomings, or hassles, but instead you will see them as a crying need that could be solved by a business you could start.

Expanding on this, you need to look at any problem you encounter in life as a need that is not specific to you, but one that is common to everyone. Unfortunately, most of us see our problems, difficulties, struggles, and tribulations as unique to us; in reality, with seven billion people on planet Earth, we need to assume that many other people have encountered this exact same problem.

A good example of this is a company that created a wristwatch that reminds Muslims of each of their five daily prayer times. This company looked at the problem of trying to keep track of these times as needing a solution.

Complete exercise 1-6 in workbook

How should the world work?

Another way to identify a need in a market that could then lead to potential business is to think about how the world should be in context of a "need" for a potential customer. Focus on your customer and envision, "What is the best way that they could have this need met?" Don't limit your thinking process; dream as big you dare and as radically as you possibly can! You'll need to expand your thinking and imagine, reflect on, and develop your thoughts regarding how an ideal world would operate as it would pertain to your product and the best possible way your customer's needs can be fulfilled.

Complete exercise 1-7 in workbook

INSIDE AND OUT: COMBINING BOTH APPROACHES

Ultimately, the best option for finding and choosing a business is to use a combination of both approaches—look outside of yourself for business ideas and then inside yourself to determine if this business aligns with:

- Your dreams
- Your life purpose
- What you enjoy doing
- What you do better than most other people
- The ability to make a living at it

If you become an expert in something that matters to people enough that they will spend money on your solution to their "problem," you have the foundation of a viable business.

Complete exercise 1-8 in workbook

IDEA SOURCES: AN ENDLESS WELL

As you implement what we have discussed thus far, the world becomes your wellspring for possible businesses. You can apply and augment this approach by considering some possible opportunities that directly present themselves to you instead of you searching for business ideas.

Current or previous employer

Is there something your current/past employer is/was not doing or addressing that could become a business? Is there a market that they are not serving? You can also look at ideas, plans, or possible businesses your employer has rejected or did not pursue. Is there a market your employer has exited or a market in which they failed that you could pursue with a different business model?

Travel

If you travel to different parts of the United States or the world, look for new and growing products in either your hometown or your destination that is not available in the other place—this could be an idea for a business. Look for ideas for products or services that could be well received in a certain geographic area that are available and in demand in another area. Have ethnic or religious groups relocated to or from a certain country or area and no longer have access to desired products or services? Both importing and exporting can be the source of possible businesses.

Information sources

Business ideas can come from reading publications or attending seminars, workshops, fairs, or conferences on starting new businesses or on buying a franchised business. Watch skills-oriented TV programs (e.g., home improvement, cooking, outdoors adventure, animal training programs) to see if there is a new market or product that could be the basis for a business.

In all of the above, consider only current and sustainable trends in the marketplace that must be present for the proper foundation of a business, not fads that will be gone quickly, thereby leaving your business adrift in a red sea of losses.

Complete exercise 1-9 in workbook

TOUGH CHOICES: PRODUCT OR CUSTOMER FIRST?

While it is better to start from an identified need for a specific target customer and then move to a product, you can have a product and then try to find a customer for it—but be aware that this is similar to trying to push a piece of string. Pulling a piece of string—finding a customer with a need and fulfilling it—is much easier.

To discover and understand who your customer is, you want to ask questions like the following:

- Who will need this product?
- Who will benefit from my product?
- Who is the product made for?
- How will it help them?
- Where do they live?
- Where do they work?
- What do they do in their spare time?
- Do they have children?
- How old are they?
- What is their gender?
- What is their income?
- How will I reach them? Do they watch TV, listen to the radio, surf the Internet, use social media?

Complete exercise 1-10 in workbook

ADVANTAGES OF OWNING A BUSINESS

Is starting and growing a business really worth the effort? Here are several advantages of owning a business:

1. You have control over the decisions affecting your life.
2. You have the creative freedom to potentially do whatever you want to do with your business.
3. You have extensive flexibility as to what your workday, work week, and personal schedule look like.

4. You obtain the personal satisfaction and pride that comes from owning a thriving and successful business.
5. You have the self-esteem that comes with operating a business that is a pillar of your community and society.
6. You gain the personal fulfillment that comes from pursuing your dreams.
7. You have a business that gives you a purpose for your life.
8. You can increase your wealth dramatically through a successful business.
9. In essence, you have complete job security and you do not have to worry about age-related job biases.
10. You can ease into retirement slowly and work the amount of hours you wish to work as you age.
11. You can possibly strike it rich by selling your business, providing you with an exit strategy and retirement lifestyle that you could not achieve otherwise.
12. You are able to tailor your fringe benefits to meet your particular needs and personally benefit from the tax laws.
13. You can benefit from the many tax advantages that are available to business owners.
14. You reap the benefits that come from strengthening your community as a result of your business being part of your community.
15. Depending on the type of your business, you obtain the satisfaction that comes from positively impacting society and the world.
16. You realize the incredible sense of satisfaction that comes from creating and providing jobs for other people.

ꝛꝛꝛ

Complete exercise 1-11 in workbook

ƧƧƧ

DISADVANTAGES OF OWNING A BUSINESS

There is a flip side to having your own business. Some disadvantages are:

1. Depending on the size and complexity of the business, the financial risk could be substantial.
2. Almost undoubtedly you will work long hours or very long hours in and on your business.
3. Because of the nature of operating a business, you will be subject to having a fluctuating income.
4. You will have to make many decisions on an ongoing basis that will affect your business and your personal life.
5. You will have to manage and cope with all of the responsibilities of running a business.
6. You will have to do things that you do not like to do because until the business becomes larger, you are ultimately responsible for everything.
7. You must be able to supervise and manage people; otherwise your business will remain you and only you.
8. You will have to deal with the pressure to produce revenue and manage the finances of your business.
9. You have to be careful to avoid "business owner burn-out."
10. You must plan for an exit strategy from your business because you cannot just retire from your business like you would retire from a job.

ƧƧƧ

Complete exercise 1-12 in workbook

MAJOR FACTORS: NARROWING YOUR CHOICES

There are a number of factors that you have to consider in choosing to start a business. I have broken these factors down into separate categories so you can consider them individually.

Do you have the temperament and personality to operate a business?

There are several sub-components that comprise this personal assessment, namely:

- **Motivation**
  - Are you a self-starter?
  - Do you have the drive and determination to run your own business?
  - Are you a driven, "Type A" person? (This trait helps but is not necessary.)
  - Are you willing to work the long hours that most likely will be necessary to make your business a success?
- **Personality**
  - Are you a high-energy person? (The higher your energy level, the better.)
  - Do you have the temperament and personality to deal with customers?
  - How confident are you in your own abilities?
  - Are you comfortable with taking risks or do you prefer the "safety" of someone else being in charge?
  - Do people naturally trust you?
- **Work Habits**
  - Are you organized or disorganized?
  - Do you follow through on tasks or do you have a large number of "unfinished" projects or tasks?
  - Do you enjoy working hard or are you not the "best" employee?

- **Control**
  - Do you like to be in charge or do you prefer to follow other leaders?
  - Do you like to make decisions?
  - Do you second-guess yourself frequently?
- **People Skills**
  - Do you like to communicate with others? How good are your communication skills?
  - Do you get along well with other people and vice versa?
  - Do you like being around people and working with people or do you prefer to work by yourself?
  - Have you supervised people before and did you like supervising them?
  - Do you have the temperament and personality to manage employees?
- **Family and Health**
  - Is your family situation and the constraints and time limitations that they present compatible with having your own business?
  - What is your health situation?

While all of the above factors are very important, I have found that if a person has a high enough drive and determination for their business, they can overcome any issues.

Where does this "overcoming" drive and determination come from? As we will learn, it comes from a dream for your business and your Vision to see that dream fulfilled. As the saying goes, "The past is a better predictor of the future than a person's intentions." If your self-assessment of the above considerations wasn't positive, it may not be the best time to start your own business.

Complete exercise 1-13 in workbook

Who will be the target customer of your business?

There are a number of questions that you must address and answer with regard to this issue:

- Who needs my product?
- What does my target customer really want?
- How will my product help my customer?
- Where will I find my customer?
- Can my customer afford my product?
- How will I differentiate my business and product from my competitors'?

Complete exercise 1-14 in workbook

What knowledge do you need to acquire?

Here are some things to think about to increase your likelihood of success at your chosen business:

- Have you thoroughly researched your target industry and business to determine what you need to know to be successful?
- Have you personally spoken to other business owners in your target market?
- Have you ever worked in a business like the one you are planning to start?
- What is your educational background? Does it give you the skills that are desirable for running a business (e.g., sales, marketing, accounting, finance)?
- Are there other people and their skill sets that you will require as an owner for your business to be successful?

Complete exercise 1-15 in workbook

How will you acquire this knowledge?

A great way to acquire this knowledge is to work in an existing business like the one you want to start. Write down your goals for working in the business so you can focus your time and take on responsibilities that will enable you to achieve those goals.

Complete exercise 1-16 in workbook

How much start-up capital will you need for your business?

Although we will cover this entire area in Chapter 8, here are some things to consider early on:

- Have you calculated realistically how much money you will need to start your business?
- How big of a business will you have in terms of employees?
- Have you roughly determined the minimum amount of sales that you will need to stay in business (i.e., your break-even point)?
- How much money have you saved that you can put into your business?
- Are these funds readily available (e.g., money market account, stocks, bonds), or are they tied up real estate or in a retirement plan?
- Do you know how much you will be able to rely on from your suppliers (i.e., their invoicing terms) for helping fund your business?
- Have you identified possible sources for obtaining additional funds to start and grow your business?

Complete exercise 1-17 in workbook

In which geographic area are you going to start your business?

- Does your customer's need for your product depend on a specific geographic location? For example, don't plan to sell beach umbrellas at the North Pole.
- Do the demographics of your customer favor a specific geographic location?
- Is the source of your product dependent on a specific geographic location? For example, if you are opening a fishing business, it probably should be located near a body of water.
- Are the demographics of a certain geographic area best for your business's growth and expansion?
- Does the availability of your needed workforce or transportation needs necessitate a specific geographic location for your business?

- Does the cost of doing business support a specific geographic area for your business?
- Do the demographic trends or other trends of a certain geographic area indicate that this area would be the best location for your business?
- Does the tax structure of a particular city, county, state, or country favor a specific geographic area for your business?
- From a geographic standpoint, do you want to be close to or far from your competitor's geographic location?

Complete exercise 1-18 in workbook

What are the barriers to entry to start this business?

Are there high or low barriers to entering your target market? For example, starting a steel manufacturing business requires large amounts of capital—a high barrier—versus the low capital, or low barrier, of starting a home cleaning business.

Having high or low barriers to entry for your target market works both for and against you—if it is easy to for you to enter a new market, it's also easy for new competition to enter the market. The opposite holds true when there are high barriers to entry—while it may be more difficult and require large amounts of capital for entry, the same holds for everyone and you will not have many competitors.

Complete exercise 1-19 in workbook

In which physical location are you going to start your business?

- If your customer will be traveling to your location, what is the most convenient location for them?
- From your customer's standpoint do you want to be in a specific location? For example, should your lunch restaurant be close to many office buildings?
- Do the traffic flows, transportation issues, parking availability, physical characteristics of the real estate, position of the actual physical location favor a specific physical location, like on a corner?

- Do the demographics of your customer favor a specific physical location—perhaps a strip mall on the way to and from a suburban area where commuters are likely to use dry cleaning services?
- Is a certain physical location best for your business's growth and expansion?
- Does the availability of your materials and supplies, needed workforce, transportation needs, utilities, etc. necessitate a specific physical location for your business?
- Does the cost of doing business support a specific physical location for your business?
- From a physical location standpoint, do you want to be close to or far from your competitor's physical location? For example, do your want to set up your jewelry store in New York's jewelry district or far from it?

Complete exercise 1-20 in workbook

NAMING YOUR BUSINESS

You want a name that captures the essence of your business or establishes a brand identity—ideally, a name that differentiates you from your competition. In deciding what to name your business you basically have three options:

1. A name that clearly identifies the nature of your business (e.g., Equestrian Supply).
2. An intriguing name that can be a play on words or have some element of cuteness to it (e.g., Jet Blue).
3. A made-up name (a word or phrase that actually means nothing) but that is meant to convey an emotion, concept, or be intriguing to the customer (e.g., Kodak).

In general, you want to avoid using your name as the business name. This tends to indicate that the business is basically you or an extension of you;

when you want to exit the business, there may be negative consequences to the operation of and valuation of the business.

Complete exercise 1-21 in workbook

TIMING ISSUES

Potential business owners often wrestle with the decision of when to start their business. They weigh the state of the economy, the financial well-being of their target customer, the availability of financing, and many other factors that affect the financial viability of a business. While these are all very important factors to consider (which we will discuss more fully in Chapter 8), you should keep in mind that many, many great businesses have been started during economic recessions or downturns (e.g., Microsoft, General Electric, FedEx) or even during the Great Depression (e.g., Hewlett Packard, Ocean Spray Cranberries, Publix Super Markets). If you have a great idea for a business or an invention that could become a business, go ahead and start the business before someone else comes up with the same idea.

One thing you should keep in mind: if your business has a seasonal component to it such as a landscaping business or a business that sells only Christmas items, you will need to build in a certain amount of lead time when determining when you want to actually start your business. It takes a period of time to get your start-up business operating; you don't want to open so late you will not capture your market for a whole year.

While starting a business during an economic downturn makes things more challenging, if you have a great idea and you pursue it by using the information and methodology in this book, most likely you will end up with a thriving business. Keep in mind that even during weak economic times, the seeds of an economic recovery are already sown.

The following six factors are always at work to create new and additional demand by your potential customer:

Everything eventually wears out and has to be replaced.

1. It is human nature to get bored very quickly with what we have, then we start to desire something new or different.
2. The attraction of new products and innovation in current products make people willing to pay for the latest product even though their prior purchase may still function satisfactorily.
3. As time marches on, all people's situations and needs change, so new needs are always being created.
4. If a new product produces future cost savings, even though an existing product may meet their needs, it would make sense to purchase a new product.
5. Population growth in the world is continually creating new consumers and new business opportunities.

Sooner or later the economy will rebound; the earlier you get your business up and running by using the guidelines in this book, the better off you will be in the long run.

Complete exercise 1-22 in workbook

TYRANNY OF THE URGENT

Let me take a few minutes to specifically address those who want to start their own business but are still employed as W-2 employees or contractors. What I call "tyranny of the urgent" is your greatest enemy! If you look at your average work week, it probably looks like this.

- Work: eight hours a day
- Commute each way and lunch: two hours a day
- Go to bed, sleep, get up: nine hours a day
- Eat: two hours a day
- Spend time with your family or friends: two hours a day

This totals 23 hours a day. Unless you utilize your commuting and lunch hours for planning, thinking, and dreaming about your business or actually working on your business, then all you have is just one hour a day and your weekends.

Weekends tend to be filled with catching up on all the things that fell through the cracks from Monday through Friday—house maintenance, family times, church or synagogue, socializing. This means if you do not focus your energy and say to yourself, "I need to set some significant amount of time aside for starting this business," the business will never happen. If you plan on just "fitting the business in" when you get around to it, the tyranny of the urgent will end up delaying or preventing you from ever starting your business. Unfortunately I have seen this situation time and time again where a person wants to be a business owner, but they make little or no progress year after year because of three things:

1. They do not set time aside to focus on their business.
2. They do not develop a compelling Vision for their business.
3. As a result of (1) and (2) not occurring, they do not end up with the "fire in their belly" that will motivate them each day to do something on their business that moves them closer to their Vision for their business.

Focus on your Vision for your business like a laser by utilizing that one hour *and* your commuting and lunch time for planning, thinking, dreaming about and working on your business.

Complete exercise 1-23 in workbook

THE BUSINESS CHOICE CHICKEN-AND-EGG SYNDROME

You now understand that there are two areas that are absolutely foundational to starting and growing a business: 1) choosing a business to start and 2) developing a compelling Vision for that business (we will talk much more about what constitutes a compelling Vision in Chapter 3).

Here is the chicken-and-egg syndrome when it comes to choosing a business: To choose a business to start you must have some kind of vision of what you want your business to look like. However, you cannot create a Vision for your business without first choosing what kind of business you want to start.

For simplicity's sake in this book, we are going to assume that you first choose a business to start and then develop a Vision for your business. But in reality, these two steps occur in such close proximity to each other that it almost does not matter which comes first.

An interactive cycle takes place between choosing a business to start and developing a Vision for your business. Once you have chosen a business and then developed an initial Vision, that Vision may affect which business you choose. This may lead you to a slightly different Vision for your business, which, in turn, may mean that in reality you are choosing a different business to pursue.

Here's an example: You decide to start a lawn maintenance business. As you develop a Vision for what this lawn maintenance business would look like, you realize you really do not want to just do lawn maintenance—you want to create new landscaping designs. This means you have now moved from being a landscaping business to being a landscaping design business. Let us suppose that as you do research into the landscaping design industry, you realize that with your engineering background you would be very good at designing waterfalls, patios, decks, water features, brick-and-stone design features, etc. The result of this research means your new Vision for your business is a "hardscape" design company, which is a different business altogether.

There is no perfect solution to this conundrum. The best alternative is to get started on your business and to be aware that you will face this cycle as you proceed.

ʓʓʓ

THE SOLUTION

As Greg and I chatted on various occasions about what was the best thing to do with his spare time in retirement and whether or not to start a business, Greg recalled the many times he had traveled to Africa on mission trips. With his engineering background, he had become intrigued with their water conservation technologies. Because of frequent and intense droughts, the people had embraced water conservation technologies that were not used extensively throughout the rest of world.

As we continued to discuss his options, Greg realized that starting a water conservation technology business would be something that he would really enjoy doing. He felt that his engineering background would serve him well; with his energetic and inquisitive mind he would be able to develop and apply new technologies. When confronted with many challenging situations in the past when he was a sales engineer, he had successfully operated on his own. He thought that owning a business would not be that much different from what he had already done.

Since he was also very people-oriented, building a business with other people would be fun. As he considered the ongoing and growing drought situations throughout the world, he realized from a financial standpoint this could be a very profitable business. It would also fit very well with his life purpose, which was to help people. Finally, he said to himself, "This is a win/win situation because besides doing something that I would greatly enjoy, I can do something that would make the world a better place."

ZZZZZZZZZZZZZZZZZZZZZZZZZZZZZZZZZZZZZZZZZZZZZ

CHAPTER TWO

Recipe For A Thriving Business

THE CHALLENGE

Sal was the owner of a large office furniture business that had grown significantly over the last several years. He now had over 25 employees. When he came to my office he was despondent. "I just want to sell the business," he said. "Tell me what it's worth."

Sal was a very creative, dedicated, and driven person who sometimes got quite frustrated with the details of managing his employees and all the minutia of running a business. Sal was in his late thirties and was recently widowed with three young daughters. His intense brown eyes at times revealed how overwhelmed he felt trying to address the myriad details involved in making sure the business stayed on target while at the same time taking care of his family.

He asked me "How do all these moving parts—having a direction for the business, keeping my customers happy, my systems running properly, maintaining a strategy for the business, making sure my employees do what they're supposed to do—fit together? I just think somebody else would be better running this business than I am. I just want to get out."

ʑʑ

RECIPE FOR A THRIVING BUSINESS

The most powerful emotional force in people's lives is their dreams. No doubt you had expectations, hopes, and dreams for your business when you started. Perhaps some of these were to:

- Create a very profitable business;
- Grow your business to 1 million, 10 million or 100 million dollars;
- Expand to multiple locations;
- Earn a comfortable living while spending plenty of time with your family;
- Create a business that you can pass on to your loved ones;
- Go public with your business;
- Sell your business for a huge profit and retire;
- Have a business that runs itself thus giving you a stress-free life;
- Control your own destiny by being your own boss.

For some business owners, some of those dreams may have come true. For others, their business just has not been what was hoped for, imagined, and counted on.

Perhaps your business has not been as profitable as you hoped, has not ended up not growing as much as you wanted. The day-to-day operations of your business have become a real hassle. Personnel problems have begun to mount. The fun that you thought you would experience from having your own business is missing. Your business is running your life instead of vice versa. You're a bit disappointed!

If any of these situations describe you, I have great news. You do not have to continue down this path of disappointment. A thriving, enjoyable, and successful business is much, much easier than you thought.

The key to having a flourishing, successful, and enjoyable business is to use a systematic approach that covers all of the bases of business. That is exactly what you will get in this book—a blueprint for achieving the dreams for your business.

Understanding How Things Go Wrong

I have worked with over 1,200 businesses during the past 17 years. Of those, the vast majority of business owners are not satisfied with their businesses. Why is that? There are many reasons, but the top five are:

1. The business lacks profits and/or growth.
2. The business takes too much time.
3. Competition has increased.
4. Running a business is stressful.
5. Running the business causes worry and fear.

Let's take a look at these one at a time.

1. Lack of profits and/or growth—The number one reason that I have observed for business owners being dissatisfied with their businesses is the lack of profits from and growth in their business. They feel they are spending all of their time in their business, working their tail end off, but profits are not sufficient to reward them for all the hard work. Alternatively for some, their business may be profitable enough, but it is just not growing; they feel like the business is treading water, stuck in the same place.

2. The business takes too much time—For many owners, their business is taking an increasing amount of time to operate. They feel like they have no time for their family, leisure, and hobbies.

3. Increased competition—Both the number of competitors and the ferocity of the competition are increasing for virtually all businesses. This is especially true if your business has an internet component—with the internet, your competition is anywhere and everywhere.

4. The stress of running a business—Operating a business is very stressful in general. When you add concerns about lack of profits, zero growth, time commitments, and increased competition, the stress mounts.

5. Worry and fear—Business owners worry to death about their businesses. They are fearful about what might catch them off guard and being unprepared.

The Solution

Whether it is disappointment with your business or outright failure, the solution to each of the above challenges is fully addressed by building your business on these four foundational principles:

1. Defining **specific goals** for your business.
2. Creating a concrete and comprehensive **strategy** for your business.
3. Developing and following through with an explicit **execution plan.**
4. Obtaining or providing sufficient capital for your business.

Why do so many business owners overlook these four basic principles? One impediment is that a business owner must first recognize that these four things are really necessary in order for their business to thrive. Some business owners say to themselves, "With so many things that I must do, what are the things that I must absolutely do versus things that I can I skip doing?" In this scenario the business owner focuses on the "urgent" concerns in their business and they end up overlooking and not addressing these four crucial principles.

Even if they do perceive that these four actions are necessary, they do not have a method, system, or blueprint for accomplishing these tasks. Without a structured approach, many business owners resort to the trial-and-error method. They try this and then they try that—and neither may work.

Furthermore, they decide to go to a seminar, read an article, or talk to a friend—and then they try to implement some of the "advice" that they received. But it does not work. The business may show some improvement, but not to the point that they anticipated—and they end up disappointed again.

As stated previously, to create a thriving business, you must follow a systematic approach that covers all the bases of your business. If any of this rings true in your business, I have some good news for you: I have only included in this book what is *truly necessary* to create a thriving business. Sure there are other things that might be nice to do or are good ideas, but will not in themselves "make or break" your business—you will not find them in this book. As you will see, there actually are not that many things that *must* be done for your business to be tremendously successful.

Also, by understanding the need for developing a compelling vision for your business, identifying your critical success factors, and then translating your vision and critical success factors to your strategy, you will create within yourself the drive, determination, or resolve to actually do the things that we will discuss. Actually *doing* these things is critical; just *knowing* them will not make them a reality in your business.

Actually *doing* these things is the execution of your strategy. As you will see, once identified, these factors become the foundation of what you are trying to accomplish in your business. Lastly, to accomplish all of the above, you must provide for the funding and financing of your business; otherwise you will end up like the proverbial person who has a great car, but has no gasoline in the tank to enable it to operate.

As you will shortly see, these four general and foundational concepts actually translate to the four specific building blocks of your business. This chapter covers the overall structure, the building blocks for accomplishing the above four foundational tasks. In Chapters 3 through 9, we examine the detailed steps for carrying out these tasks.

Persevering

A few years ago while vacationing in Ireland, I went running down by the ocean. The first leg of my run was fine—I was behind a hill that sheltered me from any wind. But then I rounded a bend on the path and was met with the full force of a gale wind coming off of the ocean. I could barely move against the wind and felt like one of those cartoon characters whose legs are moving but they are going nowhere.

Now my inclination was to stop running, give up, go back to my cozy bed and breakfast inn, and write off going for a run as a "good idea that just did not work out." However, I knew that if I just gave up, I would be very disappointed with myself for not surmounting this challenge. I knew that if I just endured the wind for a while and completed my run, I would be so satisfied with the results of my exercise that I would consider the reward worth the effort.

It is the same way with all businesses. Initially, you are going along fine and you say to yourself, "Hey, this is easy; there's nothing to this running my own business." Then right around the bend, you meet a gale force wind and your inclination may be do nothing, give up, cut corners, or just avoid the issue or situation and put this on the list of "good ideas that just did not work out."

There are many possible types of "gale force winds" that may affect your business and lead to disappointment. They may involve taking a specific action within your business. Or they may entail taking the steps (and risks) to take your business to the next level. Or the "winds" may represent dealing with some very challenging issues in your business that prevent you from making your business all that it can be.

As a potential or existing business owner, how do you overcome the "gale force winds" that will periodically or continually blow in your face? The answer is in the seven steps of creating a thriving business that are laid out in this book. But first, you must understand the components of a thriving business—what I call your Structure of Profitability.™

Complete exercise 2-1 in workbook

COMPONENTS OF A THRIVING BUSINESS

During the past 17 years, countless business owners have shared with me that they do not fully understand how all the parts of a business interconnect. What does a successful business look like? How do you grow a business? What structure is necessary to create a profitable business? What do you really need to do to develop a flourishing business? What should be the overall game plan for creating a thriving business?

My clients have found that fully understanding the four building blocks of the Structure of Profitability™ has helped them answer these questions and decide what they needed to do to take their business where they want it to go. These four building blocks provide the knowledge and insights you need to determine what must be done to create a phenomenal business.

Without the tools to understand the dynamic parts of a business and how they fit together, most business owners gravitate to the area of a business with which they are most comfortable or they know the best. For example, if their background is in accounting, they tend to focus their attention and spend the majority of their time on the finance aspect of the business. This leads to the neglect of the other areas, sometimes with disastrous results.

Let me introduce you to these four building blocks which comprise the system or methodology that we use for assessing where a business is and implementing the plans to move the business toward its goals:

1. Translate the goals of your business into an overall and compelling **vision** for your business.
2. Identify the make-or-break factors, or what I call **critical success factors,** that are unique to your business that you absolutely must do to be successful.
3. Develop a **strategy** to achieve your vision and accomplish your critical success factors.
4. Develop the systems that will enable you to **execute** your strategy.

As you will shortly see, these four building blocks correlate directly with previously mentioned four basic principles of building a successful business. Let's dig into these building blocks to lay the foundation for the rest of this book.

1. Development of a Compelling Vision for Your Business

The first building block in creating a thriving business is to answer the questions: Where do you want to take your business? What do you want your business to look like? What are your overall goals for and desired direction of your business?

This is not a pie-in-the-sky Vision, but a concrete, specific, and detailed description of what you want your business to look like. A number of self-help and personal fulfillment books talk about your destiny in life being determined by how you view yourself and where you see yourself going in life. In working with over 1,200 businesses, I have found that businesses can be thought of in the same way—the ultimate destiny of the business is determined by the business owner's Vision for the business, how they view their business and where they see it going. In Chapter 3, we will cover the entire subject of why a Vision is so crucial and how you develop a Vision for your business. This Vision is the absolute foundation of your entire business!

> **VISION**

Fig. 2-1

2. Identification of Your Business's Critical Success Factors

The second building block in producing a thriving business is to identify and define your business's unique make-or-break factors—your Critical Success Factors. Your Critical Success Factors are the things that your business must absolutely do, and do correctly, to be successful. Your Critical Success Factors are founded on the overall Vision and are identified after you have defined the Vision for your business. Graphically, your Critical Success Factors are positioned on top of your Vision. Chapter 4 discusses why your Critical Success Factors are so important and how to identify them. Your Critical Success Factors are the things on which you must focus your business's time and resources to create a successful business.

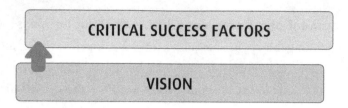

Fig. 2-2

3. Creation of an Overall Strategy for Your Business

The third building block in creating a thriving business is the development of a Strategy that addresses the three primary functional areas of a business—marketing and sales, production of your goods or services, and the financing of your business. Your Strategy for these three areas delineates the detailed plan for how your business will achieve its Vision and accomplish its unique Critical Success Factors. You develop this Strategy only after you have defined the Vision for your business and identified its Critical Success Factors.

Your Strategy and its three components graphically rest on top the Vision for your business and its Critical Success Factors. Chapters 5, 6, 7, and 8 cover the details of how to develop a strategy for each of these areas. Your Strategy is the detailed roadmap for taking your business to where you want it to go.

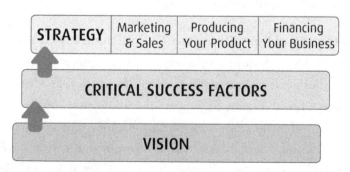

Fig. 2-3

4. Establishment of a Practical Execution Plan

The fourth and final building block in constructing a thriving business is to execute your Strategy in an innovative and systematic manner. The systematic execution of your Strategy involves the tactical and practical actions that must be accomplished to make your overall strategic plan a reality. This step also includes implementing a mindset of innovation throughout your entire business. These four elements will enable you to achieve the vision you have for your business and attain your Critical Success Factors. Chapter 9 shows you how to use innovation and systematization to separate your business from other businesses. When you combine these four building blocks into what I call the Structure of Profitability™ the entire process graphically looks like this:

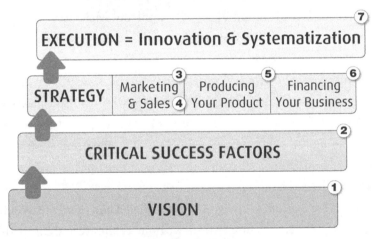

Fig. 2-4

If you closely examine the above Structure of Profitability™ diagram you will notice that there are actually seven distinct and specific steps that are contained within the four building blocks. Specifically, the seven steps are:

1. Vision
2. Critical Success Factors
3. Marketing
4. Sales
5. Producing your Product or Service

6. Financing Your Business
7. Execution

In the rest of this book we will be addressing and examining these seven steps in the above order because one step builds on the prior step, enabling you to create a thriving business.

WHY THIS STRUCTURE MATTERS

Why is the above structure important? Studies have indicated that the vast majority of a business's success is tied to proper execution of an overall plan for the business. Both Harvard Business School and McKinsey and Company studies have shown that 90% of the reasons that businesses fail are tied to failure to execute its strategy.

You cannot execute properly without having a strategy for execution. You cannot develop an effective strategy without knowing your business's unique Critical Success Factors. You cannot determine your Critical Success Factors without defining the Vision for your business and where you want to take it. This means that to create a thriving business you must put in place all four of the above building blocks for your business.

Also, because a business operates in the frenzied and dynamic world of the marketplace and its related competition, without a cohesive and comprehensive operation plan, invariably a business will fall into a pattern of reacting rather taking predefined actions that are targeted at specific outcomes. Without a comprehensive plan, most businesses end up degenerating into operating in a crisis management mode. Business owners ultimately spend their time putting out "fires" all day long or "plugging their finger in the dike" trying to solve problems. The result of operating in this fashion is that a business gets trapped in a cycle of what I call the "tyranny-of-the-urgent" syndrome, reacting and responding to daily, weekly, and monthly problems, issues, crises, and pressures. The result is that the business makes little if any progress toward its overall long-term goals and objectives.

An unintended byproduct of this tyranny-of-the-urgent syndrome is that many times both the employees and business owners begin to burn out, especially when little progress seems to occur in achieving the Vision for the business. It is emotionally, mentally, and even physically exhausting for both to the business owner and the personnel when a business regularly operates in a panic or reactionary mode. This syndrome especially causes burn out for the business owner, who ends up doing the same things day after day, week after week, month after month, and year after year, finally realizing that the business is making no progress despite all of these actions.

As you continue through this book, you will see that if you follow the steps in the above Structure of Profitability™ diagram, not only will you avoid the burn-out factor that besets so many business owners, but you will also create a business "system" that ends up maximizing your profitability and boosting the "market value" of your business.

A structured methodology can be used to create a thriving business and thereby eliminate guesswork and uncertainty. By following a systematic approach, the "What do I do next?" questions and the feeling that you just have to take a "leap of faith" to grow your business is replaced by a well thought-out roadmap for creating a thriving business.

Why is a structured methodology or a "system" of growing a business so important? Before I answer that, let me first clarify something: This book outlines a systematic approach, not a cookie-cutter approach. No two businesses will implement the concepts contained in this book in the exact same way. The reason that using a structured methodology is so important is that just like there is a natural order or progression to how our physical world or the universe operates, so there is a natural order or progression that should be used to produce a desirable and successful business. A systematic approach ensures that you do not miss any steps in developing your business, thereby eliminating the chance of overlooking something in your effort to move your business toward your expectations for today, hopes for tomorrow, and dreams for down the road.

Since enormous amounts of your time, money, effort, thoughts, and energy are going to go into your business, why not reduce the margin of error by using a systematic approach? More specifically, why would you not want to follow an approach to growing your business that eliminates the trial-and-error aspect of operating a business?

If you talk to several people who have been truly successful in their businesses, you will find that they have in some way, shape, or form done the things that are presented here. But you will also find in talking with these same people that they most likely accomplished these things as a result of years and years of trial and error. By implementing the things that are outlined in the book, you will be able to catapult your business forward because you will benefit from the secrets that your competition may or may not have discovered in their trial-and-error approach to their business. This structure will also enable you to reduce the time it will take to create a thriving business because the necessary actions are laid out clearly in a step-by-step manner.

An additional way that you will benefit from using a structured approach is if you have hit a ceiling in your business, and try as you may, you cannot punch through to grow their business to the next level. By using the methodology and techniques I cover, it will be much easier and quicker for you to break through those ceilings that may arise in your business than if you just try this and that, hoping sooner or later something will work to get you to the next level.

This chapter is only a quick summary of what we will cover in this book— many, many more concepts and ideas will be presented in the following pages. However, I must forewarn you, the concepts and ideas that are contained in this book are life changing. I promise you that if you implement this methodology and the related concepts and ideas, your business will be changed forever!

Complete exercise 2-2 in workbook

A UNIQUE METHODOLOGY

There are four unique attributes that are built into the methodology that is laid out in this book:

1. It contains a graphical way of looking at or examining a business. As we discussed earlier, many people have a difficult time getting their arms around this thing called a "business." Therefore, the methodology that

we will cover is graphical in nature so that a business owner can see a picture of how the pieces of a business fit together.

2. The methodology is built on the concept that the use of a structured approach to creating a successful business and the use of systems throughout the business are the keys to creating a business that is not overly dependent on the business owner. As you will see, using a structured approach and the use of systems throughout the business allows a business to "scale" its operations and thereby grow the business to the next level, and then the next level, and so on.

3. The concepts set forth here are not difficult concepts to comprehend, and they are very intuitive to implement. Some things in life are great in theory, but when you try to put them into practice, they are very difficult to implement. Like losing weight. To lose weight, you just must eat less and exercise more, right? Great in theory, but very difficult to implement! Other things—like quantum physics—are very challenging to understand versus something more obvious, like how to throw a ball.

Still other things in life require you to take enormous steps to start the process—a child first trying to climb up stairs or ride a bicycle. And still other things in life are so intuitive they are just like walking down a hill—all you have to do is to put one foot in front the other foot and then repeat the process.

In the same way, you will find that the concepts and methodology that are laid out here are very, very intuitive. They contain no theory that is impossible to implement, nothing that is super challenging to understand and no enormous steps that need to be taken—just small steps of figuratively putting one foot in front of the other foot.

4. The concepts, ideas, and methodology that are discussed in this book are actionable. They are not meant to be just an intellectual exercise or a project that, once completed, is cast aside as a checked-off item on a "to-do" list. Nor is what is covered something that only comes into play way down the road. As concepts are introduced, they will be

communicated in such a way that it draws you toward acting on the concept or idea, and by executing the step you will be moving closer to your goals for your business.

A TRADITIONAL BUSINESS PLAN VERSUS THE STRUCTURE OF PROFITABILITY™

What we will be discussing is very different from a traditional business plan, which is not easily implemented and many times ends up just sitting on a shelf collecting dust. This is because a traditional business plan is not actionable. However, the four building blocks of the Structure of Profitability™ and the seven steps that are comprised within this structure are actionable.

Think of these four building blocks and the seven specific steps contained within the building blocks as a traditional business plan on steroids. In other words, by utilizing the Structure of Profitability™ framework you will build your business in a better and faster way than by following a traditional business plan. These seven steps will give you and your business a very, very quick payback on your time and energy investment because you are taking actions, implementing concepts, and harvesting the benefits from these actions very quickly.

For the peace of mind of those readers who might be concerned that they might miss something that is included in a traditional business plan, I'll end this chapter showing how the methodology we will examine correlates to what is included in a typical business plan. The list below shows components of a typical business plan and after each colon are the chapter numbers and names from this book to which the items relate:

	Typical Business Plan	Chapters in This Book
1.	Describe your business:	3. Vision, 4. Critical Success Factors
2.	Define your product/ service:	5. Marketing, 6. Sales and Related Areas, 7. Producing your Product or Service

Typical Business Plan	Chapters in This Book
3. Define your target market:	5. Marketing, 6. Sales and Related Areas
4. Define your customers' needs and your ability to meet those needs:	5. Marketing, 6. Sales and Related Areas
5. Show that your customers can and will pay for your product/service:	5. Marketing, 6. Sales and Related Areas
6. Show the size of your market:	5. Marketing, 6. Sales and Related Areas
7. Understand your competitors and their strengths and weaknesses:	5. Marketing, 6. Sales and Related Areas
8. Address impediments to your success:	5. Marketing, 6. Sales and Related Areas, 7. Producing Your Product or Service, 8. Financing of Your Business, 9. Execution—the Art and Science of Innovation and Systematization
9. Describe your business's management and their expertise:	4. Critical Success Factors
10. State your marketing strategy:	5. Marketing, 6. Sales and Related Areas
11. Communicate your business's goals and objectives:	3. Vision, 4. Critical Success Factors
12. Communicate your funding needs and targeted financial outcomes:	8. Financing of Your Business

ZZ

THE SOLUTION

As Sal and I finished the meeting where we went through the Structure of Profitability™ diagram, I saw a faint smile and a look like a thousand pounds of bricks were lifted from his shoulders. I could tell by his big sigh of relief that he began to see how the elements of a thriving business come together. He said, "I get it. I now see how this thing is supposed to work and how it fits together. It just makes sense now." It was a joy to see his happiness and relief because he had been so frustrated and ready to get rid of his business because he was so stressed out.

As we worked on each element of Sal's business by utilizing the seven action steps contained in the Structure of Profitability™, his business responded well and it grew significantly. He figured out where he wanted to take the business and came to understand how to get his employees on board with this direction. He developed a Vision of where he wanted to take his business, identified his business's Critical Success Factors, created an overall Strategy for the business, and established a practical execution plan. As a result of these changes, Sal was so pleased with his business that he entered it in a small business competition, which ended up winning the local, county, and state competitions!

Because of understanding the recipe and the tools for creating a thriving business, Sal was able to see a dramatic turnaround in his business and move from having a business he wanted to sell to having a prize-winning business he was proud to own.

ZZZZZZZZZZZZZZZZZZZZZZZZZZZZZZZZZZZZZZZZZZZZZZZZ

STEP #1: VISION

THE CHALLENGE

Raul was a self-assured, intense man in his mid thirties who owned a mid-sized manufacturing business. He was driven with the desire to create a successful business. When I sat down with him in his office in an industrial park, he said "I'm so frustrated because I don't have a plan for where I want to take this business. Things are so hectic around here I don't have time to figure out what I want to do with the business and then do the planning to get there."

The following week as I met with Raul's management team, the subject of the future of the business came up. They said, "We really don't need a Vision. We just want to grow the business." I decided to explore this conversation a little further. During the following discussion it became evident that there was turmoil in the business; while they had the nice and lofty idea to "grow the business," there was no cohesive direction for make this happen, neither from Raul nor his management team. Since they had no concrete direction for the future of the business, there was no way to implement a plan for taking the business where they wanted it to go.

My challenge was to help Raul and his management team realize that having a Vision for their business was essential and critical to growing their business.

zzzzzzzzzzzzzzzzzzzzzzzzzzzzzzzzzzzzzzzzzzzzzzzz

WHY YOU NEED A VISION FOR YOUR BUSINESS

VISION

Fig. 3-1

The ultimate destiny of your business is determined by your Vision for your business. However, this is not an ethereal, fuzzy vision, but instead a concrete, specific, detailed and time-specific vision.

Your Vision defines the goals and objectives for your business, what you want to accomplish, and what you want your business to look like in the future. By identifying what you want your business to look like, you lay out the future direction for your business. Your Vision, or lack of Vision, determines the destiny of your business!

In the April 2005 edition of *Entrepreneur* magazine the author said that the number one reason businesses fail is lack of direction. That is, business owners often fail to establish clear goals. The overall long-term goals for a business are essentially your Vision for your business—what you might call your dreams for your business. Noted business planning expert and author Brian Tracy said, "All successful men and women are big dreamers . . .then they work every day toward their distant vision." Your Vision is the dream for your business you are trying to achieve. Well-known motivational and sales training speaker Zig Ziglar has been quoted as saying, "If you aim for nothing, you will surely hit it."

How do these terms "dreams" and "vision" differ? The website dictionary. com defines a dream as "a succession of images, thoughts, or emotions passing through the mind," whereas it defines a vision as "an experience in which a personage, thing, or event appears vividly or credibly to the mind, although not actually present." The dreams for your business are likely more abstract, less concrete, and less precise than your Vision for your business. It should be very concrete, tangible, specific, and sufficiently detailed.

Here are several examples of dreams for businesses and how they would translate to a Vision for each business:

Dave—Dave's Dream—Young Dave sees pictures of fine historic houses with beautiful, ornate furniture. He becomes enamored with the thought of producing elaborate furniture that many people would be able to be afford. This develops into the dream of becoming a furniture manufacturer.

Dave's Vision—Dave wants to create a furniture manufacturing business founded on a sustainable environmental model that provides jobs that pay a decent living wage for the people in third world countries who would manufacture the ornate furniture for him. This is his Vision, which actually has four parts: 1) Only wood from non-endangered tree species will be used. 2) Local artisans in third-world countries will band together to produce very elaborate, carved furniture in sufficient quantities to make Dave's business viable. 3) The local artisans will be paid a decent living wage under fair-trade concepts. 4) Dave's customers will be able to purchase very high-quality heirloom-class furniture at a very reasonable rate because of the organization that he put together.

Todd—Todd's Dream—When Todd was a boy he loved Grandma's utterly delicious cooking, even daydreaming in class about all of the wonderful smells that came from his Grandma's kitchen, the incredible tasty food she served, and how happy she made anyone who had the pleasure of eating in her house. When he told his friends about her cooking, they would say they wished they had that kind of Grandma, too.

Todd's Vision—His friends' words stuck in Todd's mind; as an adult, these dreams morphed into a Vision to create a restaurant named Grandma's Kitchen. It would use her recipes and other special dishes from bygone eras.

The kitchen would be constructed in a special way so the smells from the wonderful dishes would meet patrons as they entered the restaurant. The restaurant would be decorated like an old-fashioned country farmhouse dining room. The entire staff of Grandma's Kitchen would be trained to treat all customers like they were special guests in Grandma's house and make them want to come back every week for more of Grandma's cooking.

Laurie—Laurie's Dream—As a teenager, Laurie traveled on a family vacation to Italy where she saw exquisite Italian tile in various buildings. She nurtured the idea of bringing this kind of artistry to her own country into a dream.

Laurie's Vision—Laurie's dream eventually grew into a Vision to establish a business that includes an apprenticeship program that brings skilled tile tradesmen to her country to train unskilled people who want to become skilled "old world" tile artisans. Laurie's target market will be owners of more expensive homes who want exquisite tile work included in their homes. Because Laurie will pay the apprentices a lower wage while they are learning and being supervised by the skilled old world tile artisans, she will be able to provide the tile work at a very good price to her customers.

Complete exercise 3-1 in workbook

VISION: WHAT DOES IT REALLY MEAN?

We've talked about the dictionary definition of vision, but here's the definition as it pertains to a business: *The desired or intended future state of a specific organization or enterprise in terms of its fundamental objective and/or strategic direction.* There are much longer and more elaborate definitions of the word "vision," but this concise definition will suffice.

Let's deconstruct a few of the phrases in this definition:

- Its fundamental objective and/or strategic direction—Where is your business going? What are you aiming for? What are you trying to accomplish?

- *The desired or intended future state*—This phrase refers to the "picture" that you imagine when you envision your business some time down the road. Just how clear does this picture need to be? Very, very clear. The clearer and more specific the picture, the more powerful the Vision will be to you and all the other people who will interact with your business.

Your Vision for your business should be every bit as powerful as, for example, your childhood neighborhood memories, which you can call up in a split second. And your Vision should positively affect your emotional state in a moment, change your mood, and transport you into the future. The key to this entire process is that your Vision has to be specific enough and clear enough that it can transport you to *taste* what your business will look like in the future.

These next two concepts are unbelievably powerful and motivating:

1. Where is your business going, and
2. What will it look like when it gets there?

Everything flows from having a Vision for your business!

To develop and maintain your Vision, you must be optimistic, particularly about what your business will look like in the future. Great leaders are always optimists! Being optimistic about your business doesn't mean you are totally unrealistic or you whip yourself into a frenzy of optimism, but that you have a specific and positive dream for your business. While you may encounter trying circumstances, if you can clearly see in your mind what it will be like to achieve your Vision, you will be able to overcome these challenges.

FOUR BENEFITS OF HAVING A COMPELLING VISION

There are four benefits you will receive by having a compelling Vision for your business:

1. It becomes your North Star for guiding your business.
2. It becomes that "fire in your belly" that motivates you each day.

3. It becomes your Sales Process—A properly conceived and fashioned Vision becomes your Unique Selling Proposition.

4. It is how you deliver your product/service.

1. The Vision for your business is its North Star.

For thousands of years people have been navigating both on water and land by use of the North Star. It was a celestial beacon to guide them to their objective. They could figure out where they were and how to reach their intended destination with it.

The Vision for your business is your North Star, to guide you where you want to take your business so no matter what gets thrown at you on a daily, weekly, monthly, or yearly basis, you will not get lost or confused in the world of commerce and its competitive marketplace. Your Vision will lead you to your intended destination. Your Vision acts as a compass for your business to guide your decisions and choices on various issues, questions, and problems. Just like the North Star consistently directs its observers, your Vision always directs you to make decisions that are consistent with where you want your business to go.

2. Your Vision becomes the "fire in your belly" that motivates you each day.

Back in Chapter 2, we discussed the gale force wind that business owners may incur in moving their business forward. Each issue, each time-pressure, deadline, decision, challenge, problem, disappointment, each derailment can become part of a gale force wind blowing in your face. Sooner or later this raging wind tires you out and may lead you to get discouraged and disheartened unless you summon your drive and determination to deal with the issue *de jour*. A compelling Vision for your business becomes the drive and determination that will enable you to overcome the many challenges you will face in your business.

Having the clear picture of what you are aiming for, your business Vision becomes the fire in your belly that motivates you each day. Your Vision is why you get up each morning—to do something tangible today that will move you closer to your Vision. It will give you the resolve to meet challenges instead of avoiding the difficult decisions. Just getting busy with daily tactical activities will not take you closer to your Vision for your business. Having a concrete Vision becomes your daily motivation to do something specific to move the ball forward in order to achieve your Vision for your business.

3. Your Vision becomes your Sales Process.

A properly conceived and fashioned Vision becomes your Unique Selling Proposition. As you will see in Chapter 6, your Unique Selling Proposition is the key to your entire Marketing and Sales process.

If you properly conceive and develop your Vision, it will be so motivating that essentially all you need to do is to share your Vision with your customers and they will want to do business with you because of the "win/win" experience you will be providing them. This incredible Sales-Process side benefit of having a compelling business Vision will drive the entire Marketing and Sales area of your business. And it takes away most of the anxiety so common with business owners when the words "marketing" and "sales" are used. By using your Vision strategically in your Marketing and Sales area, you can simplify your business by letting your Sales and Marketing process be a natural outgrowth of what your business is and the "win" you are providing your customer. This approach to your Marketing and Sales area results in your Vision becoming the lifeblood of your business; however, unless you can provide your product/service to your customer, all the above is wasted effort.

4. Your Vision is how you deliver your product/service.

The fourth result of having a compelling Vision is that it shows you how to provide your product/service to your customer. When you properly conceive and develop your Vision, indigenous in this development process is figuring out specifically how you will consistently deliver your product/service to your customer. Therefore, to actually deliver your product/service—which you need to do or you will quickly be out of business—all you have to do is to move forward with the final step of your Vision. In other words, your delivery process is the execution of your Vision. We will further discuss this area in Chapter 7—Producing your product or service.

Complete exercise 3-2 in workbook

THE IMPORTANCE OF A COMPELLING VISION

A potentially overwhelming onslaught of information comes into our already busy lives from radio, television, newspapers, magazines, people, the internet, etc. This information can be separated into two basic types: actual facts and people's opinions. Marketing and advertising falls into the second category: opinions that people or businesses have.

We accept or reject factual information. And we either consciously or subconsciously accept or reject opinions. At any point in time there are a countless number of facts and people's opinions (including marketing and advertising) that impact your life as a business owner. The advertiser is promoting an agenda to make you do something they want you to do— usually to buy something. All of this input can get confusing, leaving a typical business owner unsure about what direction to take with regard to the business.

A compelling vision gives you a clear signal.

If you had a radio that picked up all the AM and FM radio signals simultaneously, your radio would be of no value to you.

However, when you tune your radio to a specific station from the entire bandwidth of radio signals, you get a clear signal. Your Vision is the one "signal" that will give you a clear picture of what you want your business to look like in the future. That is the only signal that you should be receiving in your mind and heart.

By having a focused, compelling Vision you are able to process and interpret the countless number of facts, opinions, and marketing and advertising messages that come into your life (whether you want them or not) in light of how they impact your Vision for you business. Unless you have this focused Vision, each of these inputs may cause you to say to yourself, "Well, what should I really be doing in my business"? "Maybe I should change my focus and do . . ." "Come to think about it, I really don't know where I'm going and I think I'll do what they said to do." Without a clear Vision, you could end up changing the focus for your business an infinite number of times!

Continually changing the focus for your business is like switching radio stations every second. Once again, all you would end up with is noise and not a clear, beneficial and rewarding listening experience. Only a clear, consistent Vision will move your business closer to your dreams.

A compelling vision becomes your gravity.

Another way to think about the importance of having a compelling Vision is that it functions like gravity. Specifically, if an object comes within the force of a planet's gravitational pull, then that object will be drawn toward it.

The "law of attraction" says that you will be naturally and automatically drawn to events, information, people (including customers), relationships, and activities that you perceive will move you toward your Vision. If you are not tuning into and then nurturing your Vision, then you will likely miss being attracted to those events, information, people, relationships, and activities that may enable you to reach your Vision more quickly and easily.

Use your Vision for your business as a sieve to sort through the untold inputs that come into your life. Once they have passed your selection criteria, they can be drawn into your gravitational pull and provide the opportunity to be beneficial to achieving your Vision. The end result is that once you have zeroed in on your Vision for your business, this screening process occurs automatically, without you having to even consciously think about it!

For example, suppose you feel you need some training on how to improve your marketing and sales efforts. Up to that point, you may have discarded hundreds of letters or emails on how to improve your marketing and sales processes. Once you have decided that you need additional training, you have changed your selection criterion; now, any letter, email, advertisement, discussion that pertains to how to improve your marketing and sales processes catches your eye.

The same thing will happen throughout your business once you have your Vision in place so it functions as your selection criteria, or sieve, for information. Consequently, you will select only information that is of assistance in achieving your Vision and discard information that is not germane to where you want to take your business. Now, the sixty-four thousand dollar question is, how do you develop a compelling Vision?

Complete exercise 3-3 in workbook

SOURCES OF A VISION

You may be thinking, "Okay, I can now see how having a Vision for my business can positively impact me and my business. But where does this Vision come from?" I feel there are five main sources:

1. Dreaming (or daydreaming) about a business or an invention that could lead to a business
2. Input from sources outside of yourself (reading books, listening to CD's or attending seminars)
3. Talking with other people
4. A synthesis of the above that leads to an intuitive leap of thinking
5. Dreams and visions you may have received from God—the Bible records a number of situations like this where a person received divine guidance on a subject

No matter what the source of the Vision for your business, the real issue is what your business looks like in your mind. Your task is to develop this Vision in such a way that makes it so powerful in your mind it becomes the compulsion, the drive or determination necessary to start and grow a business, deal with the "gale force wind" of issues and problems that may present themselves to you; you end up with a business that is truly worth something. Being worth something includes the financial gain from owning and operating a business as well as the personal satisfaction of running a thriving and successful business.

Complete exercise 3-4 in workbook

DEVELOPING A VISION

Let's start to put into practice what we have covered so far. I would like you to stop reading and write down your Vision for your business. There is an important reason you want to literally write down your Vision—everything in life is created at least twice. First, it is created in the mind of the creator. Second, it is created in the real world. While the subject of this book is starting and growing a thriving business, this truism that all things are created twice applies to everything, whether you are building a deck, planting a garden, cooking something, or decorating your home. Whatever you are going to do in life must be first formulated in your mind and then you can take the actual actions of creating whatever you have envisioned.

Everything *should* be created *three times*

I suggest that everything related to your business (and other things in life) should be created *three times* instead of two. Something should be first created in the mind of the creator, then secondly created physically (in our case on paper), and then thirdly created in the real world. Why? Because our minds have a curious tendency to take two or more things that do not synchronize with each other and fit them together. To you, your business may seem to be a perfect mosaic of the necessary pieces fitting together in such a way that all the "if-thens" of your business are in perfect harmony. This is because in your mind, the prerequisites of certain actions that must take place in order for your business to function properly may be accidentally glossed over.

Writing down your Vision helps to alleviate this problem. When you create something on paper, you have the opportunity to review what you are thinking about, analyze it for completeness, and look for the loose ends in your logic, actions, and goals. By writing down your Vision you may uncover any gaps in your reasoning, you will have a greater opportunity to recognize the actions that must take place for your business to be successful, and you should be able to determine the correct order in which they need to take place and thereby assess the overall realism of your plans.

Writing down everything relating to your business has two additional benefits. First, by recording everything, you will have the opportunity to revisit many of the things we will be working on in your business as you do a "first, second, and third cut" of each area. Second, you are not going to be able to do all of what is in this book in one sitting; you will want the ability to go back and review what you have recorded before and then edit it, clarify it, and improve it.

An additional step I suggest is having someone else review what you have recorded in reference to your business plans. That person should not be inclined to pour cold water on virtually any business that is being started by anyone. Conversely, you do not want an unrealistic optimist or someone who does not want to hurt your feelings by telling you the truth or who does not have the appropriate background to provide you proper feedback. Your objective should be to find someone who would give you a middle-of-the-road response that a discerning person would provide.

Complete exercise 3-5 in workbook

THREE STEPS TO CREATING A COMPELLING VISION

There are three steps in the creation of a compelling Vision for your business. We will call these "The Three C's of Visioning:

1. Conceptualizing what your business is all about
2. Creation of or crafting a compelling Vision
3. Casting your Vision

1. Conceptualizing what your business is all about

Conceptualizing is the first step and involves dreaming, thinking, envisioning, imagining, and pondering what you want your business to look like in the future. It is the "possibility thinking" in your mind and heart about what your business could be like and would be like if you could make it occur. It is a whole lot more than just wishing or hoping.

When conceptualizing what you want your business to look like, a three-year window is ideal. One year is really too short to project what your business would be, and once you get to five years, it is really difficult to imagine the details of what it might be like. A three-year model is both far enough and near enough in the future to give you the best conceptualization of what you want your business to look like.

2. Crafting a Compelling Vision

After you have figured out what you want your business to look like, you need to put this image down in words. I refer to this step as "crafting" because crafting is a more imaginative term. The goal of what I call your Vision statement is to connect with your target audience by aligning your business objectives with their personal or business goals by using words, terms, verbal pictures, and expressions that demonstrate that your business exists for them, not vice versa. You want to use language, terms, and expressions that emotionally connect with your audience so you are able to get inside their hearts and minds.

Your Vision statement should be so intriguing that it motivates people to ask, "What is this business all about?" It should be so provocative with regard to meeting the needs and wants of your target audience that they say, "Now there is a business that is trying to give me what I want." To accomplish this, you must include words and concepts that are targeted at the primary stakeholder of your business—your Customer.

Your Vision statement should be one paragraph long, and it must clearly state the "win" for your Customer for doing business with your company. Your Vision statement begins to define the goals for your business in the context of your Customer.

3. Casting your Vision

The final step of the three C's of Visioning is sharing the crafted Vision you created in the above step with your targeted audience. You can cast your Vision in many ways. You might:

- Intentionally mention it to a customer
- Discuss it with one of your employees

- Display it on your website for anyone to see
- Talk about it with a potential investor in your business

Who is your target audience to whom you should cast your Vision? Your target audience includes the five stakeholders of your business.

ʔʔ

DEFINITION: STAKEHOLDER

A stakeholder is a person or entity that has a vested interest in your business being a success. There are five possible answers to the question, "Who benefits from interactions with my business?" and these possible answers translate into the five stakeholders in your business (or any business). These are your business's possible stakeholders:

- **C**ustomers
- **E**mployees
- **O**wners and Investors
- **S**uppliers
- **S**ociety

When you put the first letters of the above together, you get the mnemonic CEOSS.

ʔʔ

Since this book focuses on newer businesses, we will deal mainly with the first and the most important stakeholder of your business: your Customer. My next book is targeted at businesses of all sizes, from start-ups to mature businesses, and covers all five stakeholders in detail.

The fact is, in working with over twelve hundred businesses over the past fifteen years, I have found that there is about an eighty-five percent success ratio of businesses that truly and consistently meet the needs of their customers. What this really means is that if you take care of meeting your Customers' needs, you have a very high likelihood of having a thriving and successful business; by meeting your Customers' needs, you as a business owner just "come along for the ride" on the shirt tails of your Customer.

While the primary target of your Vision statement is your Customer, you should think of the target audience as everyone with whom you interact. If you are excited and enthused by where your business is going (its Vision), then the people you meet in life will be drawn in by that huge gravitational pull we discussed earlier in this chapter. The gravitational pull is caused by your Vision being so attractive, so captivating, so compelling, appealing, and fascinating that someone who was not interested becomes interested. This should never be done in an obnoxious or overbearing way, but it can be easily accomplished without causing offense, as I will discuss later. Once you have figured out what your target audience's desires or needs are, you then present an attractive solution for meeting those desires. You connect with them at an emotional level (using terms, words, and concepts that they understand and to which they relate) so they will be eager and excited to purchase your product.

WHAT DOES A COMPELLING VISION LOOK LIKE?

Now that we have looked at the three C's of creating or developing a compelling Vision for your business you may be asking, "What does a compelling Vision look like?" In Steven Covey's book *The 7 Habits of Highly Effective People* the fourth habit that he talks about is "Think Win/Win." A compelling Vision has Think Win/Win at its core. You want everyone that interacts with your business—those five stakeholders—to have a win/win experience from interacting with your business.

The Primary Stakeholder: Your Customers

A business exists to serve its customers. If a business meets the perceived needs of its customers, then that business has accomplished the main task for which it exists. Therefore, your Customer automatically has a stake in your business's existence and operation. As it turns out, your Customer is by far your most important stakeholder—it is the stakeholder that will ultimately decide the fate of your business. As you will see, your "win" as the owner of your business is dependent on your Customer perceiving that they are obtaining a "win" from dealing with your business.

As we delve further into your Vision for your business, keep in mind that your Customer does not derive their "win" from your business's Vision, but from your business itself providing a product and/or an experience that they perceive as a "win" for them. The Vision for your business is the means to that end, not the end itself. The Vision is a primary tool you can use to create a business that provides and produces a "win" for your Customer.

I look at many, many Vision statements for various businesses and frequently I see only one stakeholder—the business owner—identified. An owner-focused Vision statement translates to only one big winner—the business owner. In order for your business to have its maximum chance of success, you want your business to be a win/win experience for *everyone* involved with your business (most importantly your Customer), not just the business owner.

Crucial to Customers

Your Customers should feel that by dealing with your business they will increase their likelihood of achieving their goals in life. If your target customers are other businesses, then the owners or the persons in charge of the business want to see how your business will help them reach their Vision and achieve their goals for their business. By understanding your Customer's goals for purchasing your product, you are able to build a business that focuses on enabling them to reach their goals in life as a result of purchasing your product.

Your Vision statement must clearly and unequivocally state the "win" they will receive by becoming your Customer. They must see that you as a business are useful to them or their business, your product/service is better at meeting their perceived need than your competitor's product/service, that they can trust you to deal with them in a desirable manner, and the amount they will pay you for your product/service is worth the resulting benefit. All four of these things constitute the "win" you could be providing to your Customer.

The crafting and casting of these words, word pictures, and images that show how your business will provide a "win" for your Customer are the foundation of your Vision statement, which in turn should lead to the delivery of the product that meets your Customer's needs! You can see from the above that your Vision statement is really the foundation of your business.

The Best Advertising

Word-of-mouth advertising is generally considered the most effective form of advertising. Word-of-mouth advertising is generated when you truly provide a "win" for your customer, who becomes an advocate of your business. In order for a customer to be an advocate for your business, they have to feel they had or are continuing to have a win/win experience with your business. And they must feel that this win/win experience is not just a flash-in-the pan occurrence, but that other customers can and will have a win/win experience also.

A person who recommends has nothing to gain from the experience beyond the satisfaction of helping another person get what that person wants. A strong advocate for your business creates a positive impact for your business that you should never underestimate.

Complete exercise 3-6 in workbook

THE IMPORTANCE OF A WIN/WIN EXPERIENCE

Why is win/win so important? How do you feel when you get a really good deal on a purchase? You feel like you are lighter than air, that you are so pleased with yourself for getting a great deal, that life is good and you wish every day could work out this well. You walk away knowing that you got just what you wanted and you got it a great price. You had a win/win experience; you got what you wanted and had an experience worth repeating, and the seller received your business. This is the way each person who deals with your business should feel from each interaction with your business.

Alignment of Your Vision

If you conceptualize your business in one way but you communicate your Vision in a different way, your target audience will be confused. Likewise, if you conceptualize and communicate your business's Vision in the same way, but you do not deliver on your Vision, your target audience will say, "They talked a good game, but they didn't play a good game." We will discuss this absolute need for alignment and execution of your Vision in the remaining chapters.

Complete exercise 3-7 in workbook

MISSION STATEMENT VERSUS SLOGAN VERSUS VISION

Now that you have a rough version of your Vision statement (which you will continue to refine throughout this book), you may be wondering: In what way does a mission statement differ from a business's Vision? How does a Vision statement relate to the slogan for a business?

From my perspective, a Mission statement is focused on the fundamental purpose for the very existence of the business in reference to its customers and how will it serve its customers, whereas a Vision statement is focused what the business will look like down the road in terms of how it will be meeting the needs of its targeted customer. That is the first difference.

A good analogy is that your mission is the road that your business is on, whereas, your Vision statement is the view or scenery that you see on the road. When we delve into this topic in depth in Chapter 4, you will see that your Vision statement will actually provide various views of what your relationship with your Customers looks like and how you are meeting their needs at various points in time in the future.

For instance, suppose you are on your way by car to the Florida Keys; therefore your Mission is to drive to the Florida Keys. Your Vision is comprised of the views that you will see at various mile markers as you progress to the Florida Keys—what the scenery looks like as you get to Atlanta (sunshine and warm weather), what the scenery looks like as you get to the Florida border (live oaks and pine trees), what the scenery looks like as you get to Orlando (Disneyworld®), what the scenery looks like as you get to Miami (sandy beaches and waves), and finally what the scenery looks like as you get to Key West (a semi-tropical paradise).

Lastly, how does your slogan fit in? Your slogan is the shortened version that tells others about where you are going. "I'm going to the beach" or "I'm going to the sunshine state" or "I'm going to the Keys" or "I'm going to chill out." Your slogan has to utilize terms and words your target audience understands and can relate to in an appealing manner. Your slogan provides a shorthand version of the benefit that will be obtained by your Customer from your business's operation.

An additional difference among these is that a Mission statement is entirely focused on the targeted Customer, whereas a Vision statement should address all five of the stakeholders of the business (i.e., Customers, Employees, Owners, Suppliers, and Society).

The Mission Statement as an Extension of the Vision Statement

From a theoretical point of view, the mission of the business always comes before the Vision for the business. However, in reality, very few smaller businesses have a written Mission statement. Of course the business's mission must be defined, at least in the mind of the business owner, even before the business starts; a business owner has to figure out at least in a general sense who are they going to serve. If a business is already in existence, its mission would already be identified and its Customer determined; but seldom has the mission been pinpointed and fleshed out in the form of a compelling Mission statement.

How do you translate your compelling Vision statement to a Mission statement? Take the Customer portion of your Vision statement, generalize it, and ensure that is it focused on the overall purpose of your business. That is, on which "road" is your business? A proper Mission statement is either one or two sentences long. If your Mission statement is longer than two sentences, then it is not concise enough or includes things that are not totally germane to your business's mission.

Mission statements are generally used directly with regard to your Customer. They mainly appear on marketing and sales literature, web sites, and other marketing and advertising documents. Vision statements are not generally used directly with Customers but are used behind the scenes to steer your business in the correct direction. Your Vision statement provides the focus for your entire business so everyone knows what your business is all about, and it should be the reminder to everyone in your business as to why they showed up at work and why they should give their all to your business everyday!

ꙮꙮꙮꙮꙮꙮꙮꙮꙮꙮꙮꙮꙮꙮꙮꙮꙮꙮꙮꙮꙮꙮꙮꙮꙮꙮꙮꙮꙮꙮꙮꙮꙮꙮꙮ

VISION STATEMENT

Your Vision statement is what directs and guides your business so it can meet your Customer's needs.

ꙮꙮꙮꙮꙮꙮꙮꙮꙮꙮꙮꙮꙮꙮꙮꙮꙮꙮꙮꙮꙮꙮꙮꙮꙮꙮꙮꙮꙮꙮꙮꙮꙮꙮꙮ

Complete exercise 3-8 in workbook

INCUBATING YOUR VISION

There are number of steps you can take to foster, encourage, and incubate the development of your Vision for your business.

The chief and foremost step is to focus your time, energy, and thought process on what you want your business to look like three years from now. Focusing your thought process is the key! As we discussed before in this chapter, everything in life is first created in your mind, and if your mind is not focusing on what you want your business to look like, then it is doubtful that it will happen. Related to this concept is that as you regularly think, envision, dream, and plan about what you want your business to look like, those dreams and visions become the "fire in your belly" that motivates you each day. Conversely, focusing on, nurturing, and fostering negative thoughts and doubts that you may have about your business will entirely remove the fire in your belly.

Clearing Away Negative Thoughts

It is indeed necessary to deal with and confront the negative thoughts everyone has regarding their business. The first step is to examine the assumptions, facts, and conclusions underlying your negative thoughts about your business. Why are you thinking this way? How is this affecting you? Remember that when you are overly focused on the obstacles of your business, you are not concentrating on the Vision for your business. Of course you will have issues, obstacles, and challenges in your business, but face them squarely, be brutally honest with yourself, use all the tools we will discuss in this book, and be confident that just as you cannot hold back water from eventually seeking its own course, so it is with your business; that is, if you have a plan and then consistently apply it, you will eventually reach your Vision for your business. That is because Vision is like water—it will eventually cut through anything.

Also, be aware that some or many of your concerns or obstacles and challenges in your business may just be fears in your mind, and there may not be any real support for your concerns. Past experiences may be illogically affecting your thinking. While all business owners have to deal with occasional negative thoughts, avoid dwelling on them—these negative thoughts, worries, and anxieties will become debilitating.

You need to separate actual facts from people's opinions. Be aware that most of the input you receive from other people is their subjective opinions, not true facts. Facts are irrefutable whereas someone's opinion may not be based on any factual foundation at all—their opinion is based on their interpretation of the world, which may be very different than how the real world is actually.

The best way to deal with and overcome the negative thoughts and doubts you may encounter about your business is to do the things that are presented in this book, which will give you the full assurance that you are taking the correct steps for your business to be very successful. You can also gain the peace of mind to sleep well at night knowing that you are doing all you can do for your business to be successful.

The second step related to fostering and encouraging your Vision is for you to be a laser rather than a flashlight. Both a laser and a flashlight produce light; the difference is that the laser is completely focused on a specific target, whereas a flashlight is unfocused and diffuse. You can develop a laser-like focus by using much of your free time to think about your business and how to make it an incredible success. Turn off the radio in your car and focus on thinking about your Vision and what you are going to do today to move closer to your

Vision. Or you can listen to tapes or CDs that will inspire and educate you and help you achieve your Vision.

zzzzzzzzzzzzzzzzzzzzzzzzzzzzzzzzzzzzzzzzzzzzzzzzzz

EXTRA READING

I recommend *always* having on hand some reading material regarding your business that relate to your Vision, critical success factors, goals, strategy, issues, plans, etc., so that if you have a break or you stop for a meal by yourself, you can read this information and let the Vision, critical success factors, goals, strategy, issues, plans incubate in your mind, both consciously and subconsciously, so you think of ways to accomplish these items.

zzzzzzzzzzzzzzzzzzzzzzzzzzzzzzzzzzzzzzzzzzzzzzzzzz

Complete exercise 3-9 in workbook

THREE PROBLEMS

I have typically seen the following three problems regarding the Vision for a business:

1. There is no Vision.

When there is no Vision for a business, the business just muddles along, and the business owner and other key personnel end up putting out fires all day long, doing the same activities day after day. This results in the business not moving in any meaningful direction. Because of this, the business may lose Customers and employees who decide "this business is going nowhere fast" and as a result they move on to a business that is "going somewhere."

2. There is a Vision for the business but it is not current.

In this scenario, a Vision was created for the business but the business has grown and the Vision did not evolve. Or the business made a left or right turn and the business owner simply went with the flow, not thinking about where this was taking the business and then updating their Vision accordingly. The consequence is that the Vision for the business is irrelevant to the ongoing operations of the business and the business is mostly running on autopilot.

3. The business owner creates the Vision solely, with no input from the business's personnel.

If the business only has one person or the other personnel are inconsequential to the operations of the business, then the only way the Vision can be created is the business owner creating it himself. However, if the business has other key personnel who will be instrumental in determining the destiny of the business by executing the Vision, and the business owner creates the Vision exclusively through a top-down approach, the results will be less than satisfactory.

Imagine you are in a rowboat by yourself out in the middle of a large lake, and you are rowing from one side of the lake to the other side.

Suddenly a fierce storm comes on you. You realize that your boat is going to capsize and you are going to drown because by yourself you cannot make any progress rowing against the fierce winds and waves to get to the other side of the lake. Just as you are thinking about your predicament, you look over the bow of your boat and you see that all of your key employees are in the water and they are about to drown. You then realize that if you can get them in your boat and you all row in synch to the other side of the lake, both you and they will get there safely.

It is the same with your business. If you can get your key employees involved in developing a shared or joint Vision, then you will have a much better and more complete Vision than if you do it by yourself. You want to engage the group of individuals who will be instrumental at this point in time in determining the destiny of your business. This means that as your business grows and matures, you may very well need to revisit this process with the group of individuals who at that point in time would be instrumental in determining the destiny of your business to ensure that nothing needs to be updated.

There are two reasons for engaging the crucial personnel of your business in this process. First, as the old adage goes, two heads (or more) are better than one because each person will bring their perspective on how to create a win/win experience for each of the stakeholders of your business. Then you will avoid blind spots, and the completeness and level of detail of your Vision statement will be greater than if you do it by yourself. Second, if you engage the personnel who are instrumental in determining the future of your business, the Vision becomes "their Vision" for "their company." Buy-in occurs because it is in fact their own Vision for the business. Once you have the buy-in from your key employees, who are in fact the ones who will be instrumental in determining the destiny of the business, then your key employees can obtain buy-in from the remainder of your employees.

I should mention one more benefit you will obtain from developing a shared Vision for your business: It generally produces a more harmonious and peaceful work environment because of the unifying nature of having common goals and purpose.

Complete exercise 3-10 in workbook

ᔪᔪ

THE SOLUTION

After the meeting with Raul and his management team where I laid out the concept that the foundation of any business is the Vision that the key stakeholders have for the business, a sense of order began to return to their business. They understood that creating and communicating a Vision for their business ultimately would determine the destiny of their business. As we met over the next several weeks, they were able to define a direction that truly became their Vision for the business. There was an immediate buy-in from the management team because they had helped to determine the destination for the business. Over the next several months, their Vision increasingly became the business's North Star; they used this guidance to make strategic and tactical decisions in alignment with where they wanted to take their business.

They came to realize that having a definitive Vision was paramount— and that without a Vision, they couldn't develop a strategy. During the next three months, they totally revised their sales process so it clearly presented the "win" their business was providing to their potential customers. They took their foundational Vision statement and implemented processes throughout their production and related areas to ensure that they actually delivered a win to their customers. They also took their Vision and developed a mission statement, a very catchy slogan, and began using these two tools extensively in their marketing materials. Finally, they took all the above steps and applied them to their sales processes with the result that the business grew tremendously.

ƨƨ

STEP #2:
CRITICAL SUCCESS
FACTORS AND
STRATEGY

ƨƨ

THE CHALLENGE

Ed was a happy, outgoing man in his late fifties who had a large, residential remodeling business he had started back in the 1970s. His business had grown significantly. His broad, open smile and even disposition instantly made you feel comfortable with him. His work was exclusively on expensive houses in the most prestigious part of his metropolitan area.

I worked with Ed to analyze his entire business using our Structure of Profitability™ methodology. As I met with Ed and his management team around the large, rectangular wooden table in our conference room he said, "Even though we do a very good job and have a great reputation, I feel that everything doesn't line up the way it should in our business." He went on to say "Everyone tells us that we do a great job, in a city that requires you to be top drawer; however, I think we're missing a number of things we should be doing to present a thoroughly professional image to our target customers." Of course, he could make any number of changes to his business. But what changes would actually have the biggest impact on his business and move him closer to his Vision for his business?

ƧƧ

WHAT IS A CRITICAL SUCCESS FACTOR FOR A BUSINESS?

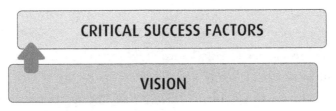

Fig. 4-1

Critical Success Factors are the items or actions that a business *must achieve* to reach its Vision and fulfill its mission. This means that your Critical Success Factors are the things that will either make or break your business. This has serious implications: the identification of and realization of your business's Critical Success Factors will ultimately determine the destiny of your business!

According to a Dun & Bradstreet study, ninety-six percent of businesses in America fail because they don't make the right decisions nor do they have the criteria to make the right decisions. The criteria for making the right decisions for your business are your business's Critical Success Factors. Noted author and speaker Tony Robbins has said that "one reason so few of us achieve what we truly want is that we never direct our focus; we never concentrate our power." Your Critical Success Factors are the things on which you need to direct your focus and on which to concentrate your power for your business!

In working with many clients over my lifetime I have seen that many business owners view the development of a detailed (not just a general "we'll figure it out as we go" type document) business strategy document or strategic plan as a daunting and overwhelming task. By using a Critical Success Factor approach to create your strategy, you are able to produce a workable and executable plan in small, easily accomplished steps compared to creating an enormous strategic plan all at once. Remember the old saying: How do you eat an elephant? One bite at a time!

The reason that determining your business's Critical Success Factors is so very important is because every business has limited resources—limited time, money, and talent. Therefore, a business must focus and channel its effort into the most important areas for that business. Utilization of a Critical Success Factors methodology will allow you to properly deploy your business's resources in ways that are focused on achieving the business's Vision most efficiently. As you shall soon see, use of a Critical Success Factor approach to determine your strategy will ensure that it can be easily implemented.

As we discussed in Chapter 3, the lack of having a Vision can lead to a business being stuck in a tyranny-of-the-urgent syndrome in which the business is just putting out fires all day long, resulting in the business going nowhere fast because it's functioning in a reaction mode instead of a strategic mode. The creation of a strategy that is based on a Critical Success Factor approach will move you from this "crisis *du jour*" mode to a strategic execution mode. And it will guide you in progressing from working *in* your business to working *on* your business.

Since your Critical Success Factors are the things that will either make or break your business, they function like a person's central nervous system. Just as your central nervous system directs the muscles of your body, so should your Critical Success Factors direct the actions of your business. Just as it directs your muscles to move in such a way to accomplish a task, so do your Critical Success Factors direct the actions of your business to accomplish each goal for your business.

The eventual outcome of identifying and achieving your business's Critical Success Factors is that your business will operate in a strategic mode instead of a reactionary mode. The result of operating strategically compare to operating tactically allows you to maximize the market value of your business because the above approach leads to having a systematized business, therefore, you will have a much better chance of creating a business you could eventually sell.

YOUR CRITICAL SUCCESS FACTORS

As we discussed above, your Critical Success Factors are the actions or objectives that are indispensable in order for a business to accomplish its Vision. The first step in determining your Critical Success Factors is to analyze your business and look for things that *must* be done correctly— if not, your business will fail—they are indispensable to your business's success. These are not just nice things to have or do in your business; they are the things that will either make or break your business. Additionally, if you accomplish your business's Critical Success Factors and everything else in your business falls apart, your business will still be successful. The next step is to examine your business and look for the things you must do well every day to be successful. This will guide you to your Critical Success Factors.

While there are many areas of a business, the four most important areas of a business for which Critical Success Factors must be identified are:

1. Marketing—How are you going to market your products/services?
2. Sales—What will be your sales process?
3. Production—How are you going to produce what you are marketing and selling?
4. Financing of your business— How are you going to finance the start-up and growth of your business?

In Chapters 5, 6, 7 and 8 we will discuss each of these areas in detail.

The next step in determining and identifying your Critical Success Factors is to record all the thoughts that come to mind when you think about the things you must do correctly in the Marketing, Sales, Production, and Financing areas of your business. At this point in this exercise, don't limit your thinking. Try to come up with as many items about which you can think.

Complete exercise 4-1 in workbook

You should end up with a fairly complete list of Critical Success Factors for your business. Now begins the process of eliminating non-critical items from the list and combining similar Critical Success Factors. The goal is between seven to fifteen. Why seven to fifteen?

Your Critical Success Factors function as your scorecard in monitoring how your business is performing. The "measurement" of how you are doing at attaining your Critical Success Factors will be translated to a measurement system (or a set of metrics) called your Key Performance Indicators. In my experience working with a number of businesses, I can validate that having seven to fifteen things for a business owner to regularly monitor in their Marketing, Sales, Production, and Financing areas is a realistic number of indicators. I have found that very rarely will a business have more than fifteen areas that are make-or-break activities.

The first step is look at each item on your list and ask yourself, "Is this something that must be done correctly otherwise it will cause my business to fail?" Is this activity indispensable to your business's success? If it is not a make-or-break item, it should be removed from the list.

The second step is to examine each of your items and determine if any can be combined. In merging two or more of your Critical Success Factors that are related to each other, you can turn them into a compound Critical Success Factor. For instance, look at these two Critical Success Factors:

- Have an effective sales process that communicates a "win" to our customers.
- Ensure that we provide proper incentives to our salespersons for using our designated sales process.

They can be combined into one Critical Success Factor:

- Have an effective sales process that communicates a "win" to our customers and includes incentives to our salespersons for using the process.

Complete exercise 4-2 in workbook

CRITICAL SUCCESS FACTOR ANALYSIS: THE FOUNDATION

By now you probably are beginning to sense how powerful it can be to use Critical Success Factor analysis as the foundation of your business. But how do you actually implement the use of a Critical Success Factor analysis as the foundation of your business? You make it your foundation by using your Critical Success Factors to develop your Strategy. Your Critical Success Factors become the supports for the structure of your business and underpinning of the entire Strategy of your business!

If you refer to the components of a thriving business shown in the Structure of Profitability™ diagram back in Chapter 2, you will see that the fourth diagram looks like the steps of a staircase. In the construction world, a set of stairs is built by first constructing the stringer. The remainder of the stairs, the stair treads and risers, is supported by the stringer. Therefore, all of the pieces of the staircase are supported by and tied together by the stringer. Think of your Critical Success Factors as the stringers that support the structure of your business, tie your business together, and, in turn, guide the day-to-day execution of your business. Just as the stringers run completely from the top to the bottom of a staircase, so it is with your Critical Success Factors—they tie your Vision to your Strategy, your Strategy to your execution, and they connect all the steps and actions that comprise your business. The role that the stringers play with a set of stairs is that they make the staircase usable. Likewise, use of a Critical Success Factors analysis approach to your business makes your business usable to the people who interact with your business.

If your Critical Success Factors span you entire business, how do you translate these factors into strategic steps? To answer that question we must first lay a little conceptual groundwork. In Steven Covey's book *The 7 Habits of Highly Effective People,* the second habit covered was "Begin with the End in Mind," and the third habit was "Put First Things First."

To begin to put the concepts that we discussed above into practice, please closely examine each of the items on the list that you have identified as your Critical Success Factors, develop a clear mental picture of what is your desired outcome, and then ask yourself, what would the result you want to achieve look like from each of the Critical Success Factors you have identified? By specifically figuring out your desired outcome for your business from each item, you are practicing "Begin with the End in Mind."

Next, separate your Critical Success Factors into one of these four categories of your business:

- Marketing
- Sales
- Production
- Financing of your business

Then, in each section arrange them by importance, with the first one being the most important step you must accomplish for your business to be successful, then the second, and so forth. By putting them in this order, you have "Put First Things First." To go up a flight of stairs you must start with the first step, then the second, and so forth; the same holds true for each of your Critical Success Factors once you have put them in the order in which they logically flow.

By doing the above, you will enable your business's Critical Success Factors to be the foundation of the Strategy for your business. Your Strategy will then lead you to systematize your business and develop innovation in your business, which will in turn guide you on a day-by-day basis in achieving your Vision for your business.

Complete exercise 4-3 in workbook

WHAT WILL THIS ANALYSIS ACCOMPLISH?

Because there are myriad demands placed on the various parts of their businesses, many times business owners do not know how to balance these demand and pressures. These competing priorities present a business owner with the dilemma of figuring out what area of their business they need to focus on, what resources to deploy in each area, and what direction they should lead their personnel. These challenges can be addressed by using your Critical Success Factors analysis. There are four things you will accomplish by using your Critical Success Factors analysis as the foundation of your Strategy:

1. Identify company-wide goals
2. Provide for the proper allocation of resources
3. Inspire and motivate your business's personnel
4. Provide ongoing guidance for your business operations

1. Identify company-wide goals.

Because your Critical Success Factors are defined as the things you must accomplish to achieve your Vision for your business, they are automatically focused on your business's company-wide goals. Alternatively, if you randomly choose goals for your business without first completing a Critical Success Factors analysis, you may end up achieving various objectives in your business, but not necessarily bringing your business closer to your ultimate objective: the fulfillment of your Vision.

By using a Critical Success Factors analysis approach, you avoid being overly focused on one or more areas of your business that are in reality not as crucial as some other areas. The result of this ill-advised focus is that you may end up neglecting areas that affect your entire business and instead concentrate on areas that only have a limited and localized impact. However, by using Critical Success Factors analysis you will concentrate your efforts on things that you have determined will affect your entire business.

2. Provide for the proper allocation of resources.

Since the Critical Success Factors approach is a holistic approach, you are examining all areas of your business to ascertain each of the "make-or-break" areas; all areas are put on a level playing field with respect to what will result in accomplishing or not accomplishing each Critical Success Factor. Hence, the allocation of your business's limited resources becomes more properly weighted than if your try to allocate your resources without first identifying your business's make-or-break areas. Conversely, if you follow "the squeaky wheel gets the grease" approach to allocating the limited time, money, and talent that your business possesses, you may utilize your resources improperly.

3. Inspire and motivate your personnel.

All people want to feel that their lives have purpose and meaning. They want to know that the work they are doing is more than just a job that pays the bills. Studies have shown that people generally want to be part of something bigger than themselves, and they want to be part of an organization that is accomplishing something significant.

Your Critical Success Factors delineate the details of what your business is trying to accomplish and what things must be done correctly every day. When your personnel become aware of your Vision for your business and your Critical Success Factors and understand what things must be achieved to accomplish your Vision, they will be inspired, motivated and challenged by their work instead of viewing their work as just being a job.

When your employees know your Vision and your Critical Success Factors, they are reminded on a daily basis: "Why did I come into work today?", "Why are we in business?", "Why are we going to all this effort to do…?", and "What are we trying to accomplish here?" This knowledge will inspire your personnel to be motivated and engaged in their work and your business because they see the big picture and realize how their efforts directly affect the success of your business. This knowledge can also foster the development of a culture of discipline in your business because employees will realize that to achieve the Vision for your business they are being requested to do certain things, in a certain way. They will be more inclined to follow company procedures and go the extra mile because they see the overall purpose of their efforts.

4. Provide ongoing guidance for your business operations.

Unless a business's daily actions are being executed based on an overall strategy, the daily ongoing operations can revert to being caught up in actions that may not be moving it toward its ultimate objective.

The business can get trapped in an endless loop of crisis management, tyranny of the urgent, and putting fires out all day long. This endless loop will not move the business closer to achieving its Vision. It also can exhaust and frustrate both employees and owners, leaving everyone involved feeling like all their activities and hard work is accomplishing little or nothing, since at the end of the day, the same issues, problems, challenges, and unmet goals that were there at the beginning of the day are still there. No real progress has been made.

By using your Critical Success Factors as the framework of your strategy for your daily operations and by allowing them to provide ongoing guidance to your business, you will ensure that you have purposeful and directed daily business operations.

SYNCHRONIZING VISION AND CRITICAL SUCCESS FACTORS

In Chapter 3, we saw how you go about creating a compelling Vision, your North Star guiding you where you want to take your business. In this chapter, we have examined how you develop the roadmap to achieve your Vision by identifying your business's Critical Success Factors.

We need to make sure the destination and the roadmap are in synch with each other. To accomplish this, you need to review your Vision statement and verify that you have identified a Critical Success Factor that relates to each of the major items in your Vision statement. If you have a major item in your Vision statement for which you have not documented a Critical Success Factor, then most likely you have omitted a Critical Success Factor from the above analysis. If that is the case, you should create an additional Critical Success Factor using the procedure outlined above.

Conversely, you may have a Critical Success Factor that does *not* directly tie to your Vision statement. This may happen since the Critical Success Factor analysis is completed at a more detailed level than the creation of your Vision statement. If this occurred, it may be perfectly acceptable; however, you should still review your Vision statement and, in light of your Critical Success Factors, determine if you need to modify your Vision statement.

Complete exercise 4-4 in workbook

MAKING IMPLEMENTATION MEASURABLE

At this point, you may be thinking about specific goals and objectives and where they fit in. They fit in here, but I avoid the terms "goals" and "objectives." Here's why:

First, we have very intentionally laid the foundation of Vision, Critical Success Factors, and Strategy so they all align with each other; the concepts of goals and objectives are already included in your Critical Success Factors. What I have found is that goals or objectives are often not necessarily tied to the overall Vision for a business—they end up being an end in themselves.

This situation may occur because business owners want to be able to see tangible results in their businesses, and so they gravitate to creating goals to have something specific at which to aim. The problem that is caused by just having goals and objectives is that they might not be at all aligned with the business's sole reason for existing—to accomplish its Vision and fulfill its Mission. This misalignment results in a business not using its limited resources in the most effective and efficient manner.

Second, because the goals or objectives may not be systematically chosen, they may not facilitate the measurement and assessment of your entire business. Concentrating on goals or objectives by themselves leads to the micro measurement of your business. Micro business measurement means setting and measuring a goal here, another goal there. However, the macro or overall measurement of how you are doing in attaining your Vision is in reality accomplished by measuring your Critical Success Factors.

This reminds me of Bob, who owned a debt collection business. He decided he would implement an incentive compensation plan that would pay his employees in part based on the raw number of collection phone calls they made. This micro measurement payment plan backfired because his employees figured out how to work the system by increasing the number of phone calls they made, which did not necessarily increase their collections. The accurate measurement that would indicate each person's productivity was collections by hour by employee. In reality it did not matter if the employees maximized their debt collections by making many short phone calls or by making fewer, but longer and more productive phone calls as long as they were able to obtain a payment from the person with whom they were speaking.

To restate it, I absolutely believe in goals and objectives and measuring how you are doing in achieving them; however, the entire area of goals and objectives for your business—and then measuring how you are doing in attaining them—is included *within* the concept of Critical Success Factors.

So instead of goals and objectives, I use the terms "Metrics" or "Key Performance Indicators" (KPIs).

Measurements

Measuring the correct things in your business and then taking actions based on those measurements provides a means of achieving your Critical Success Factors (your goals). As we have seen, the measurements you want to track should be precise measurements tied to your ultimate Vision, not just measurements for the sake of measurements. Conversely, defining your Critical Success Factors without having a method to measure how you are progressing in achieving them ends up being an exercise in futility. An example of this would be Ray with his online cleaning supply business who decided that he needed to increase the number of satisfied customers. But the question for him was how would he track the number of satisfied customers because he had no measurements of whether a customer was satisfied or not? He could have done this by:

- Using a post-sale customer survey
- Tracking his customer returns on a daily, weekly or monthly basis and then analyzing the historical trend
- Examining the number of customer service calls and their trends to determine if his customer satisfaction was improving

Before we go any further, here is a definition for the term "measurements:" Specific standards that allow for the calibration of your business's performance with regard to its Critical Success Factors.

So how do you define and monitor the proper measurements in your business? To answer this question, we must go back to the seven to fifteen

Critical Success Factors you have already defined for the following areas of your business:

- Marketing
- Sales
- Production
- Financing

Now examine each one of your Critical Success Factors and establish a scale—for instance, one to one hundred—for each item and then assess where your business is currently in the continuum of that range. You can use whatever scale is most appropriate for each of your Critical Success Factors, however I have found that a one to one hundred scale works very well.

Next, closely examine each of your Critical Success Factors and ask yourself: What is the key measurement that indicates whether or not the system, process, or function that relates to each Critical Success Factor is producing the desired outcome or output? If more than one measurement could be used as an indicator of the functioning of a system, you want to choose the measurement that is the most comprehensive gauge of the system. As you choose a measurement, keep in mind how easy it is to obtain the measurement and how reliable the measurement is. If it is at all possible, choose measurements that do not cost your business any significant amount to collect. Do not choose measurements that could be inconsistent indicators of how the system is operating.

Why are measurements so important? Let's examine more closely the purpose of measurements by looking at three truisms:

1. What gets measured gets managed and improved—If you are measuring something, you then have the information with which to manage it and improve it.
2. You cannot improve what you do not measure—Improvement suggests changing something to make it better. But if you do not

measure the initial state and the subsequent state, how can you tell if you have made it better or worse?

3. What you measure is what you get—If you do not measure the performance of your business, then you will have no way to determine if you are on the path to achieving the Vision for your business.

With no measurements, you will get arbitrary results with your business. But if you measure properly and consistently and you have the systems in place that are necessary to accomplish your Critical Success Factors and your Vision, then you will get the type of business you desire.

Metrics

Throughout the business world the term used to describe the above type of measurements is "metrics." The use of metrics allows you to establish a measurement system for your business. Metrics are measurements that effectively track performance in various areas of your business or your progress on key functions within your business (your Critical Success Factors). Metrics are the measurements used to determine if the systems you have put in place to achieve your Critical Success Factors are working correctly. Metrics are barometers used to ensure that your systems function as they are designed to function.

In Chapter 9, we will discuss how systems are critical to a business to provide a "win" for your Customer on a consistent basis. The use of systems necessitates the utilization of metrics as barometers to ensure that your systems function as they are designed to function.

Now that we have determined that you need to have metrics you can track, the next questions are:

- How often should you examine each metric?
- Should you have future projections or targets for each metric?
- If you do have future projections for each metric, at what points in time should you have a projection?

- Should all the projections have the same timeframes or dates for measurement?

Some metrics lend themselves to be measured daily, others weekly, monthly, quarterly, and still others annually. The deciding factor for the measurement timeframe for each metric is how easy it is to obtain the information. If it is simply obtained as a by-product of your accounting or operational systems—such as daily sales, daily sales order closing ratios, or daily production amounts—then daily tracking is in order. Weekly tracking of certain metrics may be most insightful for items such as sales call response statistics or quality assurance data. Other metrics may require more work to tabulate and hence lend themselves to a longer time interval, such as marketing system response results or customer service satisfaction statistics, so a monthly analysis of the metric is practical. Quarterly or annual evaluation of other metrics may be the most sensible where additional work is required to obtain the metric, such as customer satisfaction survey results or the development of new products.

Let me underscore that you need to do a realistic assessment of where your business is currently as it pertains to each one of your metrics; otherwise you are just fooling yourself. Using an unrealistic or inaccurate current appraisal of where your business is with regard to each one of your Critical Success Factors would be like measuring your house with an eleven-inch ruler to determine its square footage. If you did this, you would only be fooling yourself into thinking your house is bigger than it is.

For instance, business owners may be in for a big surprise if they assumed their employees were satisfied with their compensation simply because they did not specifically complain about their salaries or wages. These business owners may be only fooling themselves into thinking that their employees were contented. Much better indicators of the employees' satisfaction or lack of satisfaction would be to conduct employee surveys, perform exit interviews, utilize employee feedback boxes for anonymous responses, or just engage employees in conversation to determine their level of satisfaction.

With regard to future projections, yes, you should clearly have future projections or targets for each and every metric! The points in time you should have for your future projections is a function of how often you are measuring each metric—daily, weekly, monthly, quarterly, or annually. The overall process for monitoring your metrics is to assess where each metric is now, do projections of how each metric will improve based on the improvements you intend to make to your systems, measure each metric going forward at the predetermined points in time, and tabulate these metrics into your Key Performance Indicators, which show how your business is doing relative to its Critical Success Factors at certain timeframes or dates. This is your business's scorecard.

By using certain predefined dates for the evaluation of the metrics, you will have a uniform point in time across your entire business you can use to evaluate its overall performance. By periodically evaluating all your metrics at the same time, you have a non-biased assessment of how your business is performing, somewhat like the results of a footrace which records where each runner ended up compared to the winning time.

Complete exercise 4-5 in workbook

YOUR STRATEGIC PLAN: THE ROAD MAP FOR ACHIEVING YOUR VISION

Now that we have examined the first and second steps in creating a thriving business, we are ready for the third step: the development of a strategy or a strategic plan to achieve your Vision. While your Vision is the destination, or where you want to take your business, the development of your Strategy is the creation of the road map that will show you how to achieve or get to your Vision. Without a strategy or a plan of how to take your business from where it currently is to where you want it to go, you have no practical way to achieve your Vision. But first we need to define the terms "strategy" or "strategic plan."

Strategy or Strategic Plan—A pattern of missions, objectives, goals, policies, and resource-utilization plans stated in such a way as to provide a plan for a business of how to achieve its Vision and fulfill its mission. Subcomponents of this definition are:

- What line of business a company is in (this includes the product line(s), the markets, and market segments for which products are designed)
- The channels though which these markets will be reached
- The means by which the company will be financed
- The profit objectives
- The size of the organization
- The image which it will project to Customers, Employees, Investors, and Suppliers

Complete exercise 4-6 in workbook

With the above definition in mind, write down your Strategy for achieving the Vision for your business.

By writing down your Strategy, you have now taken the next step in creating a successful business! From now on I will generally use the term "strategy" rather than "strategic plan" because while the terms "strategy" and "strategic plan" basically mean the same thing, sometimes the term "strategic plan" may seem overwhelming, daunting, and too formal, whereas the term "strategy" is less intimidating and more understandable to most people.

Set this book down, take a close look at your Strategy statement you just recorded, and ask yourself: Does it address the specific things I must do to achieve my Vision? Does it enumerate all the major items that are indispensable for your business to accomplish its Vision? For a Strategy statement to be effective, it must identify a comprehensive list of the actions and activities that are imperative for you to take your business where you want it to go.

Once you have reviewed your Strategy from the above standpoint, let's take a step back for a minute. If you recall, I said that your Vision for your business guides you so you know where you are going, and your Strategy (a comprehensive, living, and executable Strategic Plan for your business) tells you how you will get there or how you will get to the goal line; that is, your Strategy is your roadmap. But exactly how do you create a comprehensive and executable Strategy for your business? As you might expect, many business owners have wrestled with this obstacle.

I feel that the huge missing ingredient in many strategies or strategic plans is that they are not established and developed based on the identification of a business's Critical Success Factors. By first identifying and addressing all your business's unique Critical Success Factors and then building your Strategy on them, you will ensure that you have developed a comprehensive Strategy for your business! Now that you have identified your business's unique Critical Success Factors, you are ready to take the third step in creating a thriving business, which is the creation of an overall strategy for your business.

We will cover the details of this step in Chapters 5 through 8 by addressing these key areas of your business:

- Marketing
- Sales
- Producing your Product or Service
- Financing

CREATING A SUSTAINABLE COMPETITIVE ADVANTAGE

For your business to thrive in the marketplace, you must develop a sustainable competitive advantage, which yields a sustainable business. Sustainability is key! To create a business that provides a better "win" experience for your Customer than your competitors provide, you must bring something else to the table that your competitors do not bring—this is your sustainable competitive advantage, which I call your "Strategic Advantage." Identifying your unique Critical Success Factors will start the process of discovering your Strategic Advantage.

This Strategic Advantage has to be provided on a consistent basis. Many businesses may provide a "win" experience sometimes, part of the time, or even most of the time. Your objective should be to provide your Customer with a "win" experience as close to *all of the time* as is humanly possible. If you only meet their needs/wants part of the time, then you are opening the door to your competitors.

You will create a business that has one or more Strategic Advantages by:

1. Using the concept of "win/win" with regard to developing a Compelling Vision for your business;
2. Coupling that with a Critical Success Factors approach;
3. Then setting goals that can be evaluated by measuring your Critical Success Factors;
4. Developing a comprehensive Strategy for your business;
5. Systematizing your business; and
6. Measuring the operation of your Systems via metrics.

The development of your Strategic Advantage(s) will in turn provide a sustainable competitive advantage for your business.

By implementing the above overall game plan for developing and casting a compelling Vision, identifying its Critical Success Factors, and developing a comprehensive Strategy for your business, you as a leader will build sustainability into your business.

We will further explore how you identify and develop your Strategic Advantage in Chapter 7—Producing your Product or Service. The identification of your Strategic Advantage and the use of a systematic approach to fully develop it will create a business that has a marketable or intrinsic value. The benefit of these actions is that they will encourage you to specifically work *on* your business instead work *in* your business and will allow you to avoid the burn-out factor that so often affects business owners.

ʒʒʒ

THE SOLUTION

As we worked together Ed realized that to properly change his business he needed to identify all the "must do's" in his business, his Critical Success Factors. He came to understand that by making Critical Success Factor analysis the foundation of his business, he could identify the entire set of his make-or-break factors. By knowing this he was able to dedicate the proper resources to specific company-wide objectives that would make the largest impact on his business. Once all of his Critical Success Factors had been identified, he shared this information with his employees, which served to inspire, motivate, and direct his personnel.

As he focused on the make-or-break factors in his Marketing, Sales, Production, and Financing areas, Ed saw significant improvements to his entire business. One of the Critical Success Factors that his team identified was that they needed to present a more professional image to their customers and the public in general. As a result of identifying this Critical Success Factor, Ed had his employees begin wearing uniforms and using company vehicles.

An additional step he took was to implement weekly project status meetings with each homeowner. Also, because his crew would be there for weeks or months on a project, they would end up knowing the customer and their tastes quite well. At the end of each job it was decided that it would be the perfect time to give the customer a nice thank-you gift. The entire area of presenting a professional image proved to be one of the business's make-or-break factors on which Ed was able to focus as a result of identifying his business's Critical Success Factors. In the end, the implementation of this and other Critical Success Factors solidified their position as a top-drawer company and enabled them to thrive in serving this market of an upper echelon of homeowners.

ใใ

Step #3: Marketing

ʑʑʑ

THE CHALLENGE

Sarah, a dedicated single mother of three who was in her late thirties, owned an energy conservation product distribution business that averaged one and a half million dollars in sales each year. She was a kind and gentle person who was extremely devoted to both her employees and customers. However, Sarah was very frustrated that her business had reached a plateau with its revenue.

She had tried various marketing programs; some were more successful than others. What Sarah found was her target markets tended to wane after a period of time due to changes in the overall economy or government tax incentives. The challenge she faced was to find consistent and growing markets where she could sell her energy conservation products and then develop an effective marketing program to reach and retain customers in those markets.

ʑʑʑ

WHERE DO MARKETING AND SALES FIT IN?

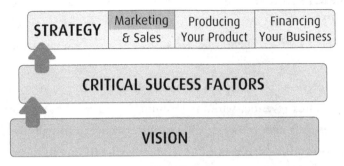

Fig. 5-1

We have completed the first two steps of the seven steps within the Structure of Profitability by laying these building blocks:

- Developing and casting a *Compelling Vision* for your business
- Identifying your business's *Critical Success Factors*

We are now ready for the third and fourth steps—your Marketing and Sales functions. Your Marketing and Sales area is part of the third building block of your business's overall Strategy. Your Marketing and Sales area sits firmly on top of your Vision and Critical Success Factors.

To recap what we have discussed so far, we have seen that everything flows from having a Vision for your business. We've concluded that this is not just something we check off of a to-do list, but instead, a compelling Vision is the factor that will drive your business forward. We discussed that you must cast your compelling Vision to your target audiences to achieve the goals for your business. Then we covered how to identify the make-or-break factors—the Critical Success Factors—for your business so you know the things that you must accomplish to achieve your Vision. Lastly, we introduced the concept of having a Strategic Plan or a Strategy for accomplishing all of the above.

We are now ready to cast your compelling Vision to your target Customer to obtain revenue for your business.

THE IMPORTANCE OF YOUR MARKETING AND SALES AREA

Why is the Marketing and Sales area of a business so important? Bill Gates, the founder of Microsoft Corporation, considers it this important: "If I only had two dollars left I would spend one dollar on PR" (PR being part of marketing and sales).

The Marketing and Sales area is absolutely imperative to your business—it is what generates revenue; without revenue, no matter how wonderful your product, your business will cease to exist unless you continually keep it afloat it with your own funds! You must generate revenue to stay in business.

Some business owners feel they have no need for Marketing and Sales efforts because their product sells itself. Unfortunately, virtually nothing sells itself. As we will see, there is always some type of marketing that has to be done to sell your product, no matter how easy it is to sell.

Many business owners undervalue Marketing and Sales and consider Production or Finance by far the highest priority area of the business. Some business owners view Marketing and Sales as a necessary evil that has to be tolerated just to be in business. The truth is that if you go to all the trouble to create a wonderful product that meets your Customers' needs or wants—but they don't know about it or you cannot convince them to buy it—then you have wasted your time and resources. The validation of a business is when a customer pays you for a product, and the ultimate validation of a business is when a customer repeats the process by paying you for your product a second, third, and fourth time.

In fact, it is very possible for a competitor's product to be inferior to your product but because they have better Marketing and Sales functions than you have, they outsell you. This may occur because your competitor has planted the perception in your Customer's mind that their product is better suited to their needs. The perceptions about a product, not the actual product, are what cause a customer to make a purchase. Therefore, it is of utmost importance to have the best possible Marketing and Sales operation for your business.

Keep in mind that everyone in your business is in Marketing and Sales in some way. Even if they are not directly employed in your Marketing and Sales areas, during the year they will talk to various people who are theoretically potential customers. You want them to tout the attributes of your products and business. This fact is another reason why, as we discussed earlier, you need to have your employees on board with your Vision for your business.

Back in Chapter 4, you identified your Critical Success Factors and you separated them into the four areas of your business. Please take a minute and review your Critical Success Factors for the Marketing and Sales area. As we work through this chapter, you will have the opportunity to update and add to the Critical Success Factors you have already identified.

While the Marketing and Sales function of a business is generally considered one area, it is in reality two separate areas that are very closely related to each other. The objective of your Marketing area's function is to bring prospective customers to you and the function of your Sales area is to actually close the sale. This chapter starts with an overview of both areas and focuses on the Marketing area for the rest of the chapter. Sales and related areas are covered in Chapter 6.

OVERVIEW OF YOUR MARKETING AND SALES AREA

When you think of your Marketing and Sales area, you should think of the word "opportunity." Opportunity is the key to your Marketing and Sales area.

The size of your opportunity refers to how large your potential market is. Determining this involves analysis of the market that presents itself to you and the solution you can provide this market. The result of this analysis determines the potential size of the opportunity that is available to your business.

Therefore, you must first determine who your Customer is and how large the market is for your product. Once you have done this, you can determine how you can take advantage of the opportunity that presents itself to you. The development of the Strategy for taking advantage of the potential market for your product and then reaching out to that market is what takes place in your Marketing and Sales area.

The formula for understanding the components of your Marketing and Sales area is:

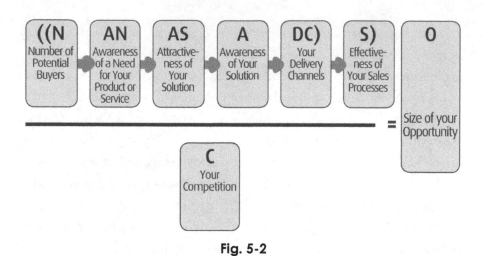

Fig. 5-2

This formula is used for two purposes:

1. To understand how your Marketing and Sales area operates.
2. To enable you to develop a strategy for generating sales for your business.

The first two of the above seven elements of this formula (Number of Potential Buyers and Awareness of a Need) pertain to the theoretical determination of how large your potential market is. The other five elements (the Attractiveness of Your Solution, Their Awareness of Your Solution, the Number of Delivery Channels You Have, the Effectiveness of Your Sales Processes, and the Number of Competitors You Have) determine how effectively you will capitalize on your market opportunity and the sales you will actually obtain.

The first four the elements of the above formula comprise the marketing area of a business. I will examine each of these components in detail in this chapter, while the remaining three elements—part of the Sales area—will be addressed in Chapter 6.

YOUR NUMBER OF POTENTIAL BUYERS

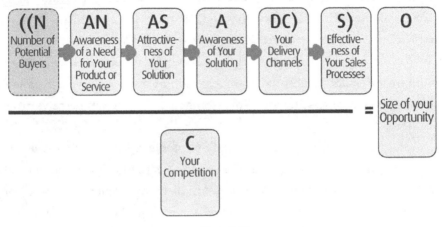

Fig. 5-3

The first step in developing your Marketing and Sales area is the determination of the size of your potential pool of customers. This assessment is comprised of two main components:

1. Determining who your target buyer is
2. Establishing your target geographic area

To determine the number of potential buyers in your market, six questions need to be answered:

1. Who is your Customer?
2. What is your Customer's perceived need and how do you determine this?
3. Are there segments to your market?
4. What segment(s) do you choose to pursue?
5. What does your Customer look like?
6. What will be your target geographic area?

1. Who is your Customer?

To determine the number of potential buyers that comprise your target market, you must first identify who your Customer is. A customer is a person or entity that has a specific real or perceived need. To figure out who your Customer is, you need to choose a group of potential Customers who have a common particular need. Your Customer in some way provides you revenue as a result of your business providing something to them that they perceive meets this need.

You can have primary and secondary Customers. Let's say that you have a manufacturer's rep business that represents construction tools and you call on Home Depot and Lowe's. You have to sell Home Depot and Lowe's on you, your business, and the products you represent to be able to place these products in the stores. However, the true Customer is the actual consumer who will purchase your products. If your products do not make the buying public happy, there is no way you can make Home Depot and Lowe's happy.

2. What is your Customer's perceived need?

A group of customers who have a common particular need is called a market. I am using the term "need" in a general sense; need includes the concept of "wants," which in actuality are not really needs, since your customer could still survive without your product; they may want it, but they do not absolutely need your product.

The next step in determining your Customer is to determine what your customer actually wants. As you start this process, keep in mind you are starting out with a presupposition based on what you currently *think* your target Customer wants; you may end up identifying a different need. There are a number of "rabbit trails" that can lead you astray in this process. Answering questions like the following will better lead you to understand what your Customer's needs or wants are:

- What is my Customer's perceived need?
- Who will need this product?
- Who will benefit from my product?

- How will my product help them?
- Why is my product important to our target buyer?
- If my product did not exist, how would it impact my target buyer?
- Are there substitutes for my product?
- Who is the ideal Customer for my product?

3. Are there segments to your market?

Now that you have identified a group of Customers who have a particular need in common and have determined who your customer is, you are ready to ascertain the potential size of your market.

First, you want to determine the existence (or not) of separate market subsegments that compromise the overall market you have identified. If the needs were fairly uniform across your potential buyers, then your target market is not fragmented (there is no market segmentation), and you can skip this step because the average Customer in your market is your target Customer. However, if you discover that the overall market is separated into various sections or pieces, then you have to decide which of the segments you will pursue.

You may quickly realize that there is a chicken-and-egg syndrome going on between market segmentation and determination of the needs of your target Customer—to identify your possible market segments you must first understand your Customers, and to understand a specific group of Customers, you must first separate your entire market of potential Customers into segments. If you preselect one segment of your potential market, then you may obtain a different definition of your Customer's needs than if you analyze all of your possible markets and unearth a different set of Customer needs that may vary based on the segments of your target market. Another term for market segmentation is "Niche Marketing." Niche Marketing is a key to the analysis of your market and the development of your Marketing and Sales area.

There can be almost an untold number of market segments. Listed below is a sample of market segmentation factors that may affect you

- Gender
- Age
- Marital status
- Family size (adults and children)
- Education level
- Total income level
- Discretionary income level
- Spending habits
- Occupation
- Industry or SIC code
- Geographical area
- Demographics/culture/religion
- Ethnic and cultural background and practices
- Social status
- Spare-time activities
- Choice of information sources (TV, radio, internet, social media, etc.)
- Tourist, seasonal, or permanent resident status
- Early adopter of new products/service (e.g., Apple® product devotees)
- Functional use of your product
- Quality/durability issues
- Need for customization
- Special needs or interests
- Other factors or special interests

4. Choosing your market segments

Once you are armed with the above customer information, you now have the information that will enable you to decide which market segments you will pursue in your Marketing and Production areas. Here are three questions you must answer:

1. How large is my target market?
2. Can they afford my product?
3. How can I identify and find them in the overall market?

You could use the market segment information from the list above to target a specific market so you could produce and sell a laptop that would provide a customer a product that would be customized to their specific needs. Once you had chosen this market segment, you could tailor your marketing to focus on this particular market segment, which would result in developing a specific market niche.

5. What does your Customer look like?

One of the first steps in creating the marketing systems and processes for your Marketing and Sales area is to develop a profile of your target customer. I have some good news for you: By completing the above analysis of 1) your customer's perceived need and how you determine what their need is, 2) if there are segments to your market, and 3) what segments to pursue, you already have a good idea of what your Customer looks like.

As you more fully understand what your Customer looks like, you will have the additional information needed to decode your Customer's motivating factors in making a purchasing decision. Another reason to determine what your Customers look like is to calculate how many of them exist, thus enabling you to ascertain the size of your potential market. An excellent way of determining this is to develop a profile of your Customer. By creating a profile of the specific characteristics common to your target Customer (market segment), you will be able to execute your Marketing and Sales operations more effectively. Please refer back to the items listed above under the heading **3. Are there segments to your market**? for the areas that could be analyzed to understand what your Customer looks like.

6. What will be your target geographic area?

The last thing that must be addressed to establish the number of potential buyers for your product is to determine your target geographic area. In the above steps, we have clarified who your target Customer is and what they look like, but to provide your product to them, you must be able to support a marketing and sales function in their geographic area, to deliver your product to them, and to provide post-sales support to them—all where they are located. Determining your target geographic area could play out in four possible ways. You could:

- Choose a market segmentation structure strictly based on the location of where your customer lives or works.
- Find that your target customer is concentrated in a certain geographic area.
- Identify the fact that a specific customer need only exists in particular locales.
- Choose to start or expand your business based on certain geographic boundaries. For instance, first you start your business in the city in which you are located, then you expand to the neighboring city, next you expand to your entire county, then you grow to serve your whole state.

What is the actual size of your market?

To determine the number of potential buyers in your market, you need to actually calculate the size of your market based on the above information. Before you proceed with your marketing effort, you need to have some idea about what price you will charge for your product. To help you figure out how to decide on price, I will borrow a concept from an economics textbook—the demand for a product depends on the price of the product. The term used to describe this economic reality is that demand is "elastic." The lower the price of the product, the greater the quantity of product you will sell; the higher the price of the product, the lower the quantity you will sell. To calculate the quantity of the product you will sell, you must estimate the selling price.

The following overall conceptual formula states that the available number of customers times the average purchase volume per year times the average selling price per unit equals your annual market potential. This conceptual formula breaks down into these six basic steps that will help you calculate the actual size of your potential market:

1. Total number of potential Customers in your target market
2. Average usage rate for your product per customer
3. The selling price of your competition's products
4. Your costs to deliver your product (we will discuss this more fully in Chapter 7)
5. Add your profit per product, based on the unique things you bring to the market and your value proposition (we will discuss these concepts later in this chapter and Chapter 6). This step will provide you with an initial estimate of your selling price. If you are already in business, then of course, you know your existing selling price.
6. Based on your selling price, the competition in your market, and the strength of your Unique Selling Proposition (see Chapter 6), calculate a realistic percentage of the market that you could obtain.

Complete exercise 5-1 in workbook

AWARENESS OF A NEED FOR YOUR PRODUCT OR SERVICE

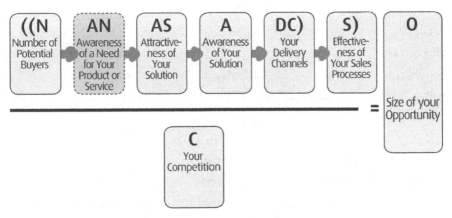

Fig. 5-4

Next you need to assess how aware your target Customer is of the very existence of your product—not your business and product, just a general awareness of the existence of your product. If your target Customer is aware of your product, your marketing and sales will be easier—all you have to do is to convince them to purchase your product instead of your competitor's. However, if your product is new to your Customer, then your marketing and sales process will be different—you must first educate your potential customer about your product, its purpose, how it will benefit them, and why they should buy it.

Here is a comparison of the two scenarios:

Aware of Product	**Unaware of Product**
Little customer education	Emphasis on education of the customer
Can use a direct selling approach	Cannot use a direct selling approach
Marketing Program is less complex	Marketing Program is more complex
Marketing Program can be less expensive	Marketing Program can be more expensive

Complete exercise 5-2 in workbook

UNDERSTANDING YOUR CUSTOMER

Once you have identified your Customer, determined the size of your market, and ascertained if they are fully or partially aware, or totally unaware of your product, you can begin to fully understand your Customer. The result is that you will be able to determine how you want to present your product to your target market.

Determine if the profile of your decision maker is different from your Customer

As you proceed with developing your marketing plan, remember that the person who will make the decision to purchase or not to purchase your product may not be the actual Customer but may be a separate person. You may be faced with a two-tracked Marketing and Sales program: one track involving trying to reach your true Customer and one track trying to reach the decision maker. Since these individuals may not be the same person, your entire Marketing and Sales area may be greatly impacted by this fact.

For instance, in purchases of children's toys, the Customer (the child) and the decision maker (the parent) are different; likewise a parent (the decision maker) buying a car for their teenage driver (the Customer). This means you must first determine which profile you need to focus on—your Customer, your decision maker, or both.

Next utilize the same process you used to develop the profile of the decision maker as you did earlier for your Customer and compare their characteristics. If they are the same, then a similar marketing strategy can be used for both individuals. Please refer to the items listed previously under **3. Are there segments to your market?** to develop the profile of your decision maker.

Once you have completed the above step, just as you did for your target Customer, an additional step that is highly desirable is to use the above profile information and other information discussed in this chapter to define who would be your ideal decision maker. But before I address the specific characteristics that make your product inviting to your Customer, we must discuss two foundational concepts.

Complete exercise 5-3 in workbook

One: Enable Customers to achieve their goals in life

Distill your solution down to this: How attractive is your product as the solution to your Customer's perception that it will meet their goals in life? These goals may be short-, intermediate-, or long-term goals.

Short-term goals are things like getting a lower rate on a credit card, buying a certain cereal that may lower cholesterol, eating at a certain restaurant tonight, buying some fashionable new clothes for your children, or buying a car polish that will make your car look more attractive.

Intermediate-term goals are things like building retirement savings, exercising more, visiting Disney World, sending your children to a private school, or buying a prestigious new car.

Long-term goals are things like financial security, better health, enjoying life, your children excelling in life, or living a certain lifestyle.

Your Customer makes their purchasing decisions based on the perception that your product will enable them to achieve their short-term, intermediate-term, and long-term goals.

If you examine the above lists closely, you will observe that they are interrelated. For instance, a lower rate on a credit card may lead to building retirement saving, which may in turn lead to financial security. Buying a certain cereal to help lower cholesterol may lead to wanting to exercise more often, which should result in better health so that one could enjoy life more. All these thoughts are running in a Customer's mind; however, many times people are not consciously aware of them, even though they are influenced by them and make choices that move toward those goals. As you will see later in this chapter, by recognizing and tying into your Customer's short-, intermediate-, and long-term goals, you will be able to layer your message and connect with them at multiple levels.

Complete exercise 5-4 in workbook

Two: Fulfill the emotional desires of your Customer

The second foundational concept is that it is not really the achievement of their goals which motivates your Customer, but the emotions they perceive they will feel when they achieve these goals. Many times your Customer is not even aware of these goals and their related emotions; they simply respond and react to these subconscious processes with conscious actions, which are all triggered by their desired emotional state. Once you understand the emotional state that your Customer wants to be in, you tap into an entirely different level of communication with and connection to your Customer. This knowledge enables you to develop your marketing program in the most effective manner.

Many businesses accidentally market their product using only the short-term goals that their product is fulfilling in their target customer's life (i.e., the wants and needs of their customer). However, to make your product more attractive to your Customer, your product should be developed and presented not only as an expression of the short-term or immediate benefits to your

Customer, but also show the long-term and overall benefits. But this must be done in a very subtle way so as not to appear to be overreaching.

One of the best ways to subtly communicate long-term goals is by using pictures instead of words. You are then allowing your target customer to translate the picture or image into a personal version of a long-term goal.

For instance, beer is marketed with the subtle message that if you buy this beer you will end up with a bunch of great friends, get a terrific-looking mate, and end up with a happy life. An SUV commercial might show a person driving all alone out west having an exciting time while climbing a beautiful rocky pinnacle, giving the subtle message that you will have an exciting and freedom-filled life if you buy their SUV.

Most people are not consciously aware of the more visceral reasons that influence them to buy various products. Generally, they are focused simply on getting their immediate perceived needs met. If you develop and market the attractiveness of your product in terms of how it helps your Customer achieve short-, intermediate-, and long-term goals and connect with the emotions your Customer associates with achieving these goals, it will greatly enhance the overall attractiveness of your product. We will continue to further apply this concept throughout this chapter and in Chapter 6 as it applies to your sales process.

Once you fully understand these emotional desires, you can understand which benefits of your product will be most appealing to your target market. Benefits are different than features: Features have no emotions attached to them, whereas benefits do. Features are generic attributes or descriptions of your product, whereas benefits are the result or outcome that a person obtains as a result of purchasing your product. Think, "four-wheel drive" versus "you will never get stuck in snow or mud;" or "side air bags" versus "your family will be safer." Compare "this disability insurance policy pays sixty-five percent of your compensation" to "with this policy you can rest assured you and your family will be able to continue living in your house for the rest of your lives." It is imperative that you describe the attractiveness of your product in terms of the benefit that will be obtained for your Customer. And you need to describe the benefits in emotional terms that have meaning to your Customer and connect you with them.

ꝣꝣꝣ

EMPHASIZE BENEFITS

Your product's benefits are the personalization of the emotional desires or emotional state that you Customer wishes to be in as a result of purchasing your product. This means that your Customer's desired emotional state should equal the benefits that your product is designed to provide to them.

ꝣꝣꝣ

Complete exercise 5-5 in workbook

Determine the buying criteria of your Customers and decision makers

To create an optimal Marketing and Sales operation, you must first fully understand both your Customer's and decision maker's motivating factors in making a purchasing choice. This motivation and rationale is known as their buying criteria. These are the factors or information on which your customer or decision maker will base their decision. Some buying criteria include:

- Is your product faster than another product?
- Is your product better than another product?
- Does your business provide better customer service than your competitors?
- Is your product less expensive than your competitor's?
- Is your product made locally?
- Does your product use "green" technology?

Just as you determined in a previous section which person's profile you need to focus on—Customer, decision maker, or both—you need to determine if you understand the goals and buying criteria of your Customer, your decision maker, or both. Many business owners get tripped up in this area because they do not ask the deeper questions regarding what motivates your buyer to make their purchasing decision. There are two levels of buying/decision-making criteria:

First level: Asking straightforward questions or looking at the obvious facts. For instance: someone who says they want to buy an automobile because it gets great gas mileage; or it has enough room for a family; or it has a high crash-safety rating. For simple products like gasoline and toilet paper, the buying criteria may not go any deeper.

Second level: Digging for deeper motivations for more complex purchases. To discover the subconscious motivating factors, you have to get to the answers to questions like:

- Why is your product important to your Customer?
- What is the true need of your Customer?
- What is the true benefit of your product to your Customer?
- What is the "win" your product is providing to your Customer?
- You provide your product so that your Customer _____ (fill in the blank)

The key is to ask the questions and then with those answers, ask questions again, and then with the next answers, ask the questions again until you have drilled down to the most basic motivating factors to get to the core need or want in your target audience. This exercise is somewhat like picking a fight with someone in order to perceive the true benefit of your product by repeatedly asking "so what" in an effort to try to perceive the true benefit of your product to your Customer. The true benefit you are trying to discover is directly related to their short-term and long-term goals.

Here is an example of this progression:

A person is buying a new front door for their house. The first reason for purchasing a door may be a physical need for a door. The next level of questions leads to the fact that they want to have an attractive yet strong front door. On further questioning you discover they want to make sure their house is safe and secure. Thereafter, you unearth that the true benefit they are seeking is physical protection for their family but one that still increases the attractiveness of their house. Finally you understand they are concerned about the home invasions they have seen reported on TV and that the long-term goal motivating them is the peace of mind that they are taking care of their family. Now you know what features about your door to promote that will assure them that the purchase of your product will accomplish this goal.

Complete exercise 5-6 in workbook

ATTRACTIVENESS OF YOUR SOLUTION

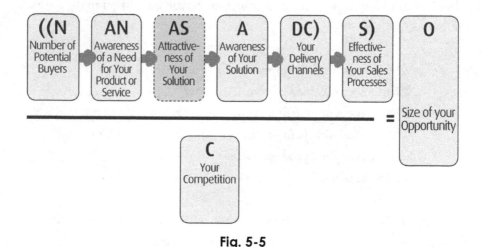

Fig. 5-5

This step involves determining how attractive your product is to your target customer in terms of the attributes of your product. This evaluation of how appealing your product is has two aspects to it. First, in an absolute sense, how alluring is your product to your Customer? Second, how attractive is your product when compared to your competitors?

The formula for determining Attractiveness of Your Solution
The formula for determining Attractiveness of Your Solution is presented on the next page.

Fig. 5-6

To position how you will market your product, you must understand each of these components. I will present each of these areas in much more detail in Chapter 7, so if you need additional understanding about these attributes, feel free to look ahead to Chapter 7. Let's examine each factor briefly here:

PA: Your Price Advantage

Your first option is to position your product as having a price advantage over your competitors, if in fact you will be selling your product at a lower price than your competitors. If you intend to focus your attractiveness on the price of your product, then you must first answer these questions:

- Do you or can you provide your product sustainably at a lower cost than your competition? If not, you are risking your business by lowering your price.
- Is your market price-sensitive? Have you done customer surveys regarding price to determine whether or not it is a significant buying criteria?

PQ: Your Product Quality

Your second option is to use the superior quality of your product or the perceived superior quality of your product as your promotional strategy.

- Is your product demonstrably better than your competitor's product?
- Have you done customer surveys regarding the quality of your product to determine if it is a significant buying criterion?

DTC: Your Delivery Time or Convenience

Your third option is to outweigh your competition in timing. If you are able to consistently accomplish this, then this could be part or all of the attractiveness of your solution.

- Is your delivery time faster or more convenient than your competitor's?
- Have you done customer surveys that determined having your product more quickly or more conveniently is a significant buying criterion?

CS: Your Customer Service

Your fourth option is to build your Marketing and Sales strategy on the claim that your customer service is better than your competitor's.

- Is your customer service better than your competitor's customer service?
- Have you done customer surveys to determine if providing a higher level of customer service is a significant buying criterion?

PU: Your Product Uniqueness

Your fifth option is to base your Marketing and Sales strategy on some unique feature of your product. The uniqueness of your product can manifest itself in several ways.

- Does your product have patent or copyright protection and is, therefore, legally unique?
- Does your product have an actual design feature that makes it different from its competitors?
- Alternatively, you could promote some attribute of your product that is not actually unique, but your competitors have not chosen to use this particular feature in their promotional strategy—therefore your product would be perceived as being unique, when

in actuality the only thing that is unique about your product is
your marketing strategy.

- Using the words "new and improved" or similar terms can also be a
variation of "uniqueness" because the product is a new or improved
version.

Complete exercise 5-7 in workbook

CREATE EXPERIENCES WORTH REPEATING

Almost as important as meeting or fulfilling your Customer's perceived need
is the overall experience they encounter in having their need met. We have
all had many experiences where our wants or needs were met, but the overall
experience ranged from less than desirable to awful: the fast food restaurant
that was anything but fast although we did eat; the car repair that cost us more
than the car was worth although the car now runs again; the home repair job
that had to rerepaired; the vacation experience that was anything but relaxing;
the tool or appliance purchase that didn't solve the problem; the meal at a fine
dining restaurant that was fine food but not much else.

Your offer of an ultimate attractive solution is one that meets the
immediate need of your Customer, moves them closer to their long-term
goals in life, and in their mind is an overall experience that, if they have the
need again, they would want to repeat.

zzzzzzzzzzzzzzzzzzzzzzzzzzzzzzzzzzzzzzzzzzzzzzz

WORTH REPEATING

From a Customer standpoint, the bottom line goal of your business
should be to create experiences worth repeating! This concept of
creating experiences worth repeating is the most powerful concept
known to the business world, and if you practice it consistently, your
business will become a world-class business.

zzzzzzzzzzzzzzzzzzzzzzzzzzzzzzzzzzzzzzzzzzzzzzz

Applying the above concepts

The summation of the above discussion is that you want to use the following five possible attributes of your product to determine what makes your product most attractive to your Customer:

1. Your Price Advantage
2. The Quality of Your Product
3. Your Delivery Time or Convenience
4. Your Customer Service
5. The Uniqueness of Your Product

Once this is done, you can and should then build your entire Marketing and Sales operation on this analysis. This detailed analysis of your product and how it enables your Customers to reach their goals in life should be done so accurately that you could reduce your entire marketing program to the "attractiveness" that you have discerned, and your business would still thrive.

As you will see in Chapter 7, this identification of what elements make your product desirable is referred to as your "Strategic Advantage." A validation of the attractiveness of your product is that if you gave a free sample of your product as part of your marketing effort, would your potential buyers want to purchase your product? For instance, if you were a restaurant, you could give a free sample of some of your dishes; if you were are car dealer, you could let someone drive one of your cars for a day; or if you were a professional, you could give a free consultation where you actually delivered a service to your Customer, not just made a sales pitch to them. In essence, you should be so confident of your product that your Customer should be able to sample your product for free and verify that your product is as good as you say it is. Conversely, the marketing technique known as bait and switch, where a Customer is lured under false pretenses, is the exact opposite of this complete honesty and transparency that I refer to here.

Sometimes businesses do not know what makes a product attractive or unattractive to their Customer. Many times you can just ask Customers,

"What do you want?" and then provide this "want" by using the above product differentiators. Another way to research and analyze product differentiators is to visit businesses in your same industry in another city or state (so there are no competition issues) and discuss what is working or not working for them, to discover possible product differentiators.

It is paramount to understand what your Customer finds attractive, because once you know this, you can also alter or revise the attractiveness of your solution; that is, you can actually change your product's attributes. Alternatively, as we discussed earlier in this chapter, instead of changing your product, once you know what makes a product appealing to various different Customers, you could refocus your existing product to a new or different market segment by applying your product's differentiators to a different market.

Complete exercise 5-8 in workbook

THEIR AWARENESS OF YOUR SOLUTION

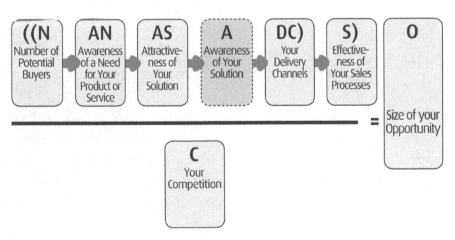

Fig. 5-7

The fourth element that comprises your Marketing and Sales Area involves the development of your overall marketing plan. The purpose of developing a comprehensive marketing plan is to ensure that your potential Customer is aware you provide a solution to their need. There are many books and seminars completely devoted to this subject; in this section we will discuss the foundational pieces of your Marketing Program to introduce you to the concepts you need to fully understand and apply. From a strategic point of view, this section is intended to outline what factors should be addressed to create an effective Marketing operation.

Listed below are the five basic actions that need to be completed to have an effective Marketing Program or marketing function. We have already covered actions one and two in this chapter. Actions three and four will be covered in the next two sections, and action five will be discussed at the end of Chapter 6.

1. Determine if the profile of your decision maker is different from your Customer
2. Determine the buying criteria of your customers and decision makers
3. Create your value proposition
4. Construct a brand identity
5. Ensure that you meet and exceed your Customer's expectations so that you have repeat sales and obtain referrals

ƨƨ

MARKETING VS. ADVERTISING

How is marketing different from advertising? Advertising is a single component of marketing. Advertising is the most visible—and generally the most expensive—component of your overall marketing plan. Your marketing plan is like the overall game plan for winning a football game, whereas advertising is a single play or a sequence of plays in the overall game plan.

ƨƨ

Create your value proposition
Your value proposition is built on The Attractiveness of Your Solution. It defines the unique value that your business and your product offer to your Customers. Your value proposition is why your Customers will want to do

business with you. It establishes how you propose to utilize the resources of your business to deliver superior value to your Customers.

ꝛꝛꝛꝛꝛꝛꝛꝛꝛꝛꝛꝛꝛꝛꝛꝛꝛꝛꝛꝛꝛꝛꝛꝛꝛꝛꝛꝛꝛꝛꝛꝛꝛꝛꝛꝛꝛꝛꝛ

ATTRIBUTES TO PROMOTE

The attributes that determine the Attractiveness of Your Solution, which are tied to the emotional outcome your Customers desire (your product's benefits), are what you should use to promote and sell your product.

ꝛꝛꝛꝛꝛꝛꝛꝛꝛꝛꝛꝛꝛꝛꝛꝛꝛꝛꝛꝛꝛꝛꝛꝛꝛꝛꝛꝛꝛꝛꝛꝛꝛꝛꝛꝛꝛꝛꝛ

This step of defining your value proposition pulls together four foundational concepts that we discussed in the Attractiveness of Your Solution section. The first of these concepts is that you must enable your Customer to achieve their goals in life. This concept is the bedrock foundation of your value proposition.

Second, you need to fully understand the desired emotional state of your Customer, the Customer's decision-making criteria; stress benefits not just features to connect at an emotional level to your Customer.

Third, you have to figure out which of the five elements (price, quality, convenience, customer service, uniqueness) you are going to use to make your solution attractive to your target Customer.

Fourth, you must design and build your whole business and its processes so that your Customer's entire experience in dealing with your business is so good that they cannot wait to do it again—you must create an experience worth repeating.

With these four steps, you have laid the foundation for defining your value proposition, why people should want to do business with you. Your value proposition is utilized to attract customers (which is marketing) and to generate revenue (your sales function) by framing your communication to your Customer is terms of benefits for them.

Here are three examples of strong value propositions and one weak example:

Strong—We provide top-quality heating and cooling solutions, tailored to our customers' needs, which are a great value and are supported by outstanding customer service so that our customers can enjoy all the quality of life that comes with having a comfortable living environment.

We provide high-quality and convenient canine training, daycare, boarding, grooming, products, and related services that are industry-leading and uniquely tailored to our customers in order for them to experience the joy of having an affectionate, well mannered and enjoyable canine companion, which will result in a lifetime of wonderful memories for our customer with their dog.

We provide high-quality workforce and work-flow systems analysis, design and implementation services customized to our customers' specific needs to create a fully engaged work force so our customers operate in the most efficient manner, thereby enabling them to achieve their business goals and maximize their profitability.

Weak—We sell all-natural body care products and give ten percent of our profits to not-for-profit organizations.

The first three relate to features that are meaningful to the customer and may result in fulfilling their needs. The last is too generic in its description and, while donating to a nonprofit is admirable, is more about the company than the customer and the customer's needs.

As we will see in Chapter 6, your value proposition enables the creation of your Unique Selling Proposition, which summarizes the actual selling strategy you will use to convince your Customer to purchase your product.

Complete exercise 5-9 in workbook

Construct a brand identity

The textbook definition of a brand is the name used to identify and distinguish a specific product or business. A brand is the overall image or value statement you are trying to create in the market for your product or business. Your brand is what you want to be known for. It is what you want to be identified with in your Customer's mind. Another way of saying this is that your brand should be what you are famous for, such as the best hamburger in town or having phenomenal customer service.

Why is having a brand image important? Developing and communicating a brand reduces the perceived risk to your Customer of making a choice to purchase your product. In making a purchasing decision, the outcome to a Customer of purchasing your product, in terms of reaching their goals in life and obtaining their desired emotional state, is never one hundred percent certain. With brand identity, your Customer will feel that since your product or business is a known commodity, buying your product reduces the uncertainty and risk they face compared to the greater uncertainty they may face in purchasing another product.

To create a brand identity, you start with the development of a psychological connection of your product or company to your market. This psychological brand identification is created in the mind of your target audience by your marketing program. Its intention is to create the expectation in your Customer's mind that your product is more desirable or is better suited to their needs than that of your competition.

Creating a brand identity continues on to the actual delivery of the experience that you have marketed to your Customer on behalf of your product or business. This experiential aspect includes the combination of all interactions with your business or its product. This is what is known as their brand experience.

The power of branding is that it sets an expectation of the experience with your product or business in your Customer's mind. This expected experience reduces the risk in your Customer's eyes. If this expected experience becomes a known commodity in the marketplace and it is a desirable experience, you are able to catapult your product or company ahead of your competition.

This is important because everything in life involves risk: the risk of taking a shower in the morning is that you could slip and fall, the risk of driving to work each day might be the possibility of getting into an automobile accident, the risk of drinking a cup of coffee at work could be the chance of spilling the coffee and scalding yourself. Each of us wants to reduce the various risks in our lives.

The objective of developing your brand is to create the impression in your target audience's mind that your brand's product has certain qualities or characteristics that make it special or unique. Keep in mind that as we discussed above, there are only five possible attributes that you can utilize to construct your brand image:

1. Your Price Advantage
2. The Quality of Your Product
3. Your Delivery Time or Convenience
4. Your Customer Service
5. The Uniqueness of Your Product

The intended outcome of creating brand recognition on behalf of your business or product is that it becomes much easier to increase your target audience's Awareness of Your Solution when they have positive brand identity firmly etched in their minds. The creation of a brand is dependent on all the concepts we have covered thus far in this chapter. This means in order to construct a brand image you must actually have a product or business that has legitimacy in supporting the brand you are trying to develop. You cannot just create a desirable brand image without having some substantiation that your product or business surpasses or is better suited than your competitor's product or business. There are five steps to fully developing a brand:

1. Determine your intended brand identity or brand image.
2. Validate your brand identity by asking questions of your prospects and customers.
    -   What do they think about when they hear or see your business or product brand?
    -   How do they perceive your brand?
    -   How do they describe your business or product brand to others?

3. Fully develop your branding by making changes based on the previous validation step.

4. Determine how you want to communicate your brand to your target audience.

5. Implement the marketing and promotion of your brand throughout *all* your marketing materials and efforts.

Complete exercise 5-10 in workbook

UPDATING YOUR CRITICAL SUCCESS FACTORS

Back in Chapter 4 you identified the Critical Success Factors for your business. Now that you have completed analyzing your Marketing area, review and, if necessary, modify and/or add to the Critical Success Factors you have already identified.

ʑʑ

THE SOLUTION

The first task that Sarah and her marketing personnel had to tackle was to determine who was going to be their target customer. Which market segments did she really want to pursue?

As we worked on her business she began to understand the components of her Marketing area, which enabled her to narrow down her potential market to the most inviting and attractive market segments. By indentifying her targeted market segments, she could determine the size of the opportunity, begin to forecast and predict her future sales, and then build a business to support those sales.

After several conversations with me, she realized that many of her potential customers were not even aware of the existence of her product. So the next thing Sarah did was to create marketing materials to educate her potential customers in each market segment about the benefits of her energy conservation products. Thereafter, she was able to place herself into the minds of her customers and try to understand their desire for energy savings. This enabled her to develop the attractiveness of her products as the solution to their high-energy consumption costs. By understanding her customers' decision-making criteria, she was able to design a marketing approach that emphasized the reasonable price of her product, its high quality, and its unique energy-saving attributes.

Lastly, she created an effective marketing program and the related materials that communicated her value proposition to her potential customers through mailed marketing material, e-mails, and follow-up telephone calls. She incorporated what she had learned previously—that until she had three marketing communications to her potential customer, she had virtually no sales. However, if she communicated the same marketing message three times over a six-month period, the response rate to her marketing increased dramatically. By considering all of these factors, she eventually created a robust marketing system that moved her business forward.

ʑʑ

STEP #4:
SALES AND
RELATED AREAS

zzzzzzzzzzzzzzzzzzzzzzzzzzzzzzzzzzzzzzzzzzzzzzzz

THE CHALLENGE

Sam, a jovial and outgoing man in his late fifties, had a big problem in his family's large printing business. A number of salespeople were quite ineffective in selling his products. While he had excellent marketing materials, he did not have an effective sales process. He had largely left the details of the sales process and techniques up to each salesperson to figure out independently. This resulted in a frustrated group of family business owners who saw much of their marketing expenses being wasted because their salespeople did not readily close sales.

This lack of closed orders caused each salesperson's commissions to be lower than they should have been, which in turn caused a morale and turnover problem in his sales force. Because Sam had felt that the problem was his salespeople's lack of motivation, twice in the past Sam had fired his entire sales staff and started again with a whole new sales team. Sadly, Sam ended up with the same ineffective sales results because the problem was not his sales personnel, but the lack of an effective sales system.

ZZZZZZZZZZZZZZZZZZZZZZZZZZZZZZZZZZZZZZZZZZZZZZZZ

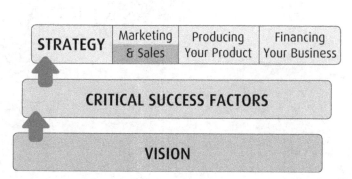

Fig. 6-1

In Chapter 5 we focused on the marketing area of you Strategy. In this chapter, we will build on the concepts that have been introduced as they apply to you actually closing a sale and dealing with the issue of competition.

YOUR DELIVERY CHANNELS

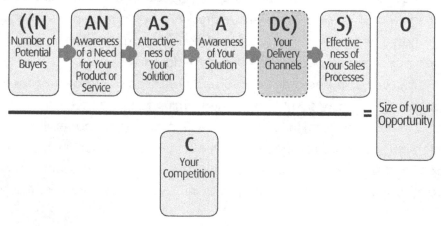

Fig. 6-2

Your delivery channels are the methods by which you deliver or distribute your product to your Customer. It is important to note that there are several terms that are used for delivery channels. Sometimes these are called your "sales," "marketing," or "distribution" channels. All of these terms refer to how your product will be provided to your Customer; we will use the term "delivery channel." Whatever wording is used, your delivery channels are the methods that you use to get your product to your Customer.

For instance, you could ship your product directly to a Customer, they could pick it up at your location, they could buy it from a store to whom you initially sold your product at wholesale prices, or, if applicable, they could download your product from your web site.

This step involves the assessment of how are you providing your product to your target Customer and determining if you should increase, decrease, or change your delivery channels?

You have to develop your marketing function before you can actually have a Customer to whom you need to deliver your product, so the concept of delivery channels sits after your Marketing components near the end of your Marketing and Sales area.

To recap, here are the steps that have been covered to develop your Marketing area:

1. Determine the need you are going to fulfill—who your Customers are and the number of potential buyers in your market.
2. Assess the awareness of a need for your product or service.
3. Develop the attractiveness of your solution to their perceived need.
4. Create an awareness of your solution in your buyer's mind.

Now you are ready to determine which delivery channels you will use to provide your solution to your Customer. While the actual development of your delivery channels rests at the end of your Marketing and Sales area, you may have conceptualized your delivery channel methodology as part of your "solution." In fact, your delivery channel could be a part of the foundation of your Vision for your business and could be the key to your solution—the unique part of your business that makes you stand out from your competitors.

Furthermore, the delivery channels that you utilize may be tied directly to be being able to fulfill your Customer's goals, impacting the actual attractiveness of your product as a result of its delivery time or convenience or uniqueness. An example of this would be a business model built entirely on buying stamps over the Internet versus going to a post office.

Keep in mind that just because the work of determining the number of delivery channels you have comes near the end of your Marketing and Sales area does not mean that it is less important than the previous steps. In fact, the previous steps in this chapter just set the stage for delivering your solution to your Customer.

Your Delivery Channel is how you physically distribute your product to your Customer. This includes physical delivery channels (mailing something versus picking something up at your location) or marketing-type delivery channels. For instance, marketing-type delivery channels might involve doing direct sales to your Customer or developing, working with, and supporting a network of distributors. The more delivery channels you have, the more sales you can have by providing the same product to your Customers via multiple and alternative means.

For instance, the soft drink Coca-Cola® is delivered (sold) to their Customers in three basic ways:

- Bottles, cans, or other containers purchased at stores
- Fountain drinks purchased at restaurants, sporting events, or similar places
- Bottles, cans, or other containers purchased via vending machines

Consequently, the Coca-Cola® bottling company can easily obtain additional revenue from the sale of one product, the Coca-Cola® soft drink, because it has multiple delivery channels. We have all seen this when a physical retail store chain establishes an online retail presence to obtain additional revenue from selling essentially the same products they sell in their physical stores; it is just being delivered via a different channel.

ƧƧ

DELIVERY CHANNEL OPTIMIZATION

In considering your delivery channels, examine your business model and ask yourself if you are properly utilizing all the appropriate delivery channels available to you.

ƧƧ

There are two decisions that involve this delivery channel area. First, which is the best and most appropriate delivery channel for your product? Second, which additional delivery channels justify their cost? Because there are additional costs to develop and maintain each delivery channel, you must compare your incremental revenue to your incremental costs to verify that the effort of creating additional delivery channels makes sense.

There is an added factor that must be considered when you explore using additional delivery channels—will the marketplace be confused by the use of the additional delivery channel so the overall message of your solution becomes distorted? This issue of confusion is what Starbucks Coffee® faced when it introduced its VIA® product for making coffee at home compared to the product that was being delivered through its retail coffee establishments. That is, would VIA® be viewed as an alternative to going to a Starbucks Coffee® location and therefore cannibalize its sales, or be viewed as another delivery channel of the Starbucks Coffee® product and thereby grow overall sales?

Besides the additional revenue, there are two related secondary benefits that using multiple delivery channels can bring to your business. First, the same marketing efforts can be used to promote and drive multiple delivery channels. For instance, a television advertisement for a physical store can have a web site listed at the bottom and the words "shop online at" added at the end of the commercial. Second, there is potential for a spillover effect when promoting one delivery channel when the same product can be purchased from a different delivery channel than the one being promoted in the advertising. For instance, a soft drink advertisement shows the soft drink being served at a cool, relaxing, and pleasant pool party, which would encourage sales from a physical store delivery channel for take-home consumption. On a different occasion, the consumer passes a vending machine in the middle of a hot city, they remember the advertisement showing the pleasant pool party, and they purchase the same soft drink via a different delivery channel (the vending machine) because of the image that has been set in their mind.

The determination of the delivery channel for your product and the possible use of multiple delivery channels are influenced by the following factors:

- How your Customer has traditionally purchased your product
- The physical attributes of your product
- Technology involving the delivery of your product
- The amount of risk involved in the purchase (e.g., buying potato chips, which could easily be sold via a vending machine, compared to an automobile purchase)
- The demographics/culture/religion of the purchaser
- How you are able to reach the decision maker
- The motives of the purchaser
- The purchaser's perceptions about your product
- The ability of and knowledge of the purchaser
- The attitudes toward your product
- The lifestyle of the purchaser
- How opinion leaders shape your market
- How people's roles and family influences affect various delivery channels
- The social class of the purchaser
- The culture and subculture of the purchaser

The bottom line of completing the above analysis is that to maximize your revenue, you want to consider and possibly choose all the delivery channels you have available to you and those that will provide you with the largest sales volume.

Complete exercise 6-1 in workbook

EFFECTIVENESS OF YOUR SALES PROCESSES

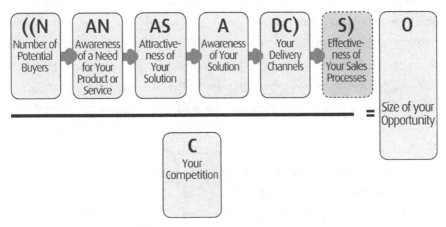

Fig. 6-3

This step involves developing an effective sales function and includes systematizing your sales processes as well as assessing the ability of your entire sales function in converting potential buyers into Customers.

Determining and developing the Effectiveness of Your Sales Processes is the last piece of assessing how large an opportunity of which you can avail yourself (your entire Marketing and Sales area) because you have to figure out the prior five steps before you can construct your sales process. The five prior elements we have examined all fall squarely within the marketing arena because they take place before you can close a sale. Once you have done the work to analyze your market and position your product via marketing, you are now ready to actually complete a sales transaction.

How Marketing and Sales relate

Marketing and Sales go hand in hand—marketing sets the stage for Sales, whereas Sales actually presents "the play" on the stage that has been set.

Without an effective sales function, your marketing efforts may be next to worthless. Conversely, without an appropriate marketing function to create the proper mindset in your Customer's mind, your sales operation will be much less effective.

The first five elements of the Marketing and Sales area we discussed so far in Chapter 5 and in this chapter are the equivalent of setting the table for a meal. You could have the most ornate, attractive, and inviting table setting, but if you never actually prepare the food for the meal, then the desired outcome of enjoying a scrumptious meal will never be achieved. This means you could have the most compelling, engaging, and effective marketing effort, but if you have an ineffective sales process, you will not obtain your desired sales. If you are in fact a start-up business, remember getting and keeping your first Customer is the most important thing you can do; once you have landed that first Customer, you can apply all the concepts in this book to get and keep your second Customer, your third, etc.

Sales uses many of the same building blocks that Marketing uses; however, sales utilizes and applies them in an interpersonal way compared to the mass media approach of marketing. Sales activities could include sales calls, presentations and meetings, networking events, etc., which engage you with your target Customer on a personal level. As we saw above, Marketing is more strategic, whereas Sales is more tactical and involves actual one-on-one interaction (interpersonal or electronic) with the Customer.

Bad news: Your Customer is a walled city.

Each Customer has, on some level, a defensive wall to protect against invasion from various sales efforts. The size of anyone's protective wall depends on many factors, including:

- Their current emotional state
- How much they trust the salesperson
- The nature of the product being sold
- The size of the claims made in the sales process
- The level of familiarity with knowledge about the product

- The strength of the desire they have for the product
- Their past experience with salespeople in this area or products of this type

Marketing does not encounter the same resistance that the sales process does because 1) good marketing is very subtle and even entertaining, so it generally is not viewed as invasive; and 2) marketing is not interpersonal whereas sales is. How does your business overcome this wall? You can't take a Customer's wall down—instead, you need to connect with your target Customer so that the wall will come down itself.

The height and strength of this wall is determined by many factors including the temperament, personality, upbringing, the nature of your Customer, and the setting in which they find themselves. Thinking back to the factors that determine the size of a person's wall, a person who would generally be considered very cynical would have the highest and strongest wall; their wall would be the most difficult to overcome.

An individual's wall is overcome at the emotional level by immediately connecting with them on something of emotional importance to them before going into the details of your sales presentation.

Continuing with the wall metaphor, there are three steps to use to scale the wall of your Customer:

1. Erect a ladder to get over the wall. This ladder consists of the following: in your sales presentation presenting the short-term, intermediate, and perhaps long-term goals of your Customer. You may want to reread the section in Chapter 5 titled "Enable your Customers to achieve their goals in life."

As we will see, by stating the goals of your Customers with regard to a possible purchase of your product, you identify and connect with them and show that you understand their needs. As a result, you are viewed as being on their side, not the adversary trying to make them do something they do not want to do. So many salespeople look at Customers as existing for them, when in reality it is vice versa—you and your business exist to meet *their* needs or goals. The bottom line is that Customers will make their buying decisions on their perception of your product's ability to take them where they want to go in life; that is, its ability to enable them to achieve their goals.

2. Carry up the "ladder" the benefits or the emotions that your Customers perceive they will feel when they reach their goals. This is the step where you really connect at an emotional level. We discussed how to identify these benefits or the emotions back in Chapter 5 in the section titled "Your product's benefits— the emotional desires of your Customer."

3. Use your product's features, characteristics, and attributes, as identified in Chapter 5 in the section titled "The formula for determining Attractiveness of Your Solution," as the grappling hook that enables you to get over your Customer's defensive wall. Present your product's features, characteristics, and attributes in a way that demonstrates to your potential Customers how your product will enable them to reach their goals and achieve their desired emotional state. Then you need to connect all three steps in your sales presentation.

The key missing piece in so many sales processes is connecting at an emotional level (either positive or negative emotions) with Customers. The result of this connection is that you will be able to get over their protective wall and cause them to take down the barriers erected to keep you an outsider.

Another way of looking at the sales process is that it a transfer of emotions. In other words, you transfer the positive emotions and excitement you have for your product to your Customers. This transfer results in them seeing the possibilities that their goals and the emotional state they wish to be in can be achieved in the same way you do.

To develop the most effective sales process, you need to build it on the foundation of understanding and meeting the emotional state related to or as a result of your Customer reaching or achieving their goals in life, couched in an overall "experience worth repeating." That is why having the knowledge of both your Customers' goals for purchasing your product and the emotional state they desire to attain can help you to:

1. Build and create a product that meets your Customers' needs
2. Increase the appeal of your product through your Marketing effort
3. Understand and connect with your Customers via your Sales process

THE CUSTOMER'S PERSPECTIVE

In marketing and sales, use the word "I" as little as possible. "I" frames something from your perspective. You need to frame your product with regard to your potential Customer's emotional world. Present the attractiveness of how your solution fulfills their need or want in words and concepts that emotionally reverberate throughout the mind, heart, and soul of the Customer.

Your Unique Selling Proposition

An outcome-based sales approach is very successful because it identifies the need, lack, want, or desire that a potential Customer is feeling and presents a solution for the emotional outcome being sought. The most effective process I have found to accomplish this in a systematic manner is to develop and utilize your product's Unique Selling Proposition (or USP).

Your Unique Selling Proposition systematizes the selling strategy you will use to convince your Customer to purchase your product. It is in essence your sales pitch. But it is not just any sales pitch. It is a sales pitch that has been clearly thought out to fully resonate with your Customer. Your USP utilizes the previously described Customer Profile and Buying Criteria to understand what motivates your target Customer to purchase your product. It uses your Value Proposition to determine what your product provides that will motivate your Customer to purchase your product. It frames your entire presentation in terms of your product's emotional benefit to your Customer.

To develop your Unique Selling Proposition, once you have a thorough comprehension of the goals and desired emotional state of your Customer and a complete understanding of the market trends that are affecting your Customer, you will need to identify the following:

- A detailed list of the major *features* of your product
- An awareness of the *uniqueness* of your product
- A recognition of the *usefulness* of your product to your Customer
- A selling proposition that conveys with *simplicity* how your product meets the goals and the desired emotional state of your Customer
- Observed or documented *results* from your Customer's use of your product

Your Unique Selling Proposition identifies and conveys four things to your Customer:

1. Your Big Idea
2. Your Big Benefit
3. Your Big Promise
4. Your Proof of Your Claims

1. Your Big Idea—Your Big Idea is a theoretical or hypothetical statement that captures the mind and imagination of your target Customer and gets that Customer excited. Your product is not Your Big Idea because your Customers are not buying your product for the product itself, they are buying it to reach their goals in life and the emotional state they feel they will be in when they achieve their goals.

Your Big Idea should be an idea or concept to which people aspire or a big-picture type statement that will capture the imagination of your audience. It should draw them into the thought "What would the world look like if _____?"

Your Big Idea is outcome-based. It opens the door to the next step, the Big Benefit. Your Big Idea is a statement that says, "Think about this concept as if you could wave a magic wand and you could experience it as if it were real." For instance, "What if exercise was fun?", "What if you could make everyone your friend?", "What if we were able to operate the world using renewable energy?" or "What if you could find your ideal soul mate?"

To create a Big Idea statement you first must have:

- A thorough comprehension of the *goals* and *desired emotional state* of your Customer
- A complete understanding of the *market trends* that are affecting your Customer

What you want to do is to plant the seed in their mind that their dream could come true.

During the above process you want to select the goal that you feel will most resonate with your target Customer and fully develop it into your Big Idea. Your Big Idea will become the "ladder" you will use to get into the "walled city" of your Customer.

Complete exercise 6-2 in workbook

2. Your Big Benefit—The next step is to take this theoretical Big Idea and personalize it by assuming it is a reality, then ask yourself, "If this Big Idea were an actuality, how would it specifically benefit my Customer?" In this step, you are now beginning to connect with Customers at an emotional level in terms of the outcomes that your target Customer desires from your product. The Big Benefit needs to be personalized and speak to the things that are important to your target Customer at the emotional level.

Using the above examples of Big Ideas, their Big Benefits would be: "If exercise was fun I would exercise regularly and look and feel great", "If I could make everyone my friend, I would be incredibly happy, I could not wait to meet the next person in my life, and I would eagerly awaken every day", "If we were able to operate the world using renewable energy we could virtually eliminate pollution, enable all the people of world to improve their lives, and alleviate many of the financial, political, and military stresses in the world" or "If I could find my ideal soul mate my life would totally be worth living, every day would be paradise, and I would want to spend every minute in joyful happiness with that person." Your Big Benefit is what you will carry up your "ladder" in order to get into the "walled city" of your Customer.

To develop your Big Benefit you must have:

- A thorough comprehension of the *goals* and *desired emotional state* of your Customer
- A complete understanding of the *market trends* that are affecting your Customer
- A recognition of the *usefulness* of your product to your Customer
Complete exercise 6-3 in workbook

3. Your Big Promise—The third step in developing your Unique Selling Proposition is to define your Big Promise—the specific thing that your product will provide to your Customer with regard to the above Big Benefit. It is very important that you identify a Big Promise that is close to or similar to your Customer's imagined Big Benefit. This makes your Big Promise as powerful as possible, which in turn increases the effectiveness of your entire Unique Selling Proposition.

Please remember during this analysis that the goal is that your Customer's desired outcome from purchasing your product should be your Big Benefit. What you are trying to do is to subtly and in a non-patronizing way tap into your target Customer's hopes and dreams, because, as we discussed back in Chapters 3 and 4, hopes, dreams, and vision are incredibly motivating factors in our lives. To be effective, your Big Promise must be significant, important, or attractive enough to motivate a person to take action but still believable enough to not raise doubts. Here are some sample Big Promises: "Our program will make exercise fun and you will look forward to it each day," "Making and keeping friends will be as natural as breathing," "Our system will make renewable energy so inviting that everyone will want to use it" or "You will stop sleepwalking through life because you find your ideal soul mate."

Your Big Promise is the "hook" you use to get over the wall of your Customer once you have carried your Big Promise up your ladder.

To create your Big Promise you must have identified and developed all the items below:

- A detailed list of the major *features* of your product
- An awareness of the *uniqueness* of your product
- A recognition of the *usefulness* of your product to your Customer
- A selling proposition that conveys with *simplicity* how your product meets the goals and the *desired emotional state* of your Customer

Complete exercise 6-4 in workbook

4. The Proof of Your Claims—The last step in developing your Unique Selling Proposition is to identify the Proof of Your Claims—the documented results that Customers have obtained by using your product. These results could be in the form of testimonials, reported results from Customers, Customer statistics, or surveys that support your claims that relate to your Big Promise. The Proof of Your Claims can also be statements you make regarding your observation of the results of Customers using your product. To support the Proof of Your Claims you must have:

- Observed or documented *results* from your Customer's use of your product

Here are some sample Proof of Your Claims:

- Ninety-five percent of our Customers who used our program report continuing to exercise at least three times a week for the next five years.
- Surveys have shown that our Customers double their number of friends within one year.

- Our Customers report that switching to renewable products made them feel they are enabling mankind to survive forever.
- Our Customers regularly share with us that they have found their "soul mate" as a result of using our service.

You know the math concept that the shortest distance between two points is a straight line; well, the shortest distance between you and your Customer is your Unique Selling Proposition. By utilizing this concept, you will have your most efficient Marketing and Sales Program. It will produce the greatest sales results on the most consistent basis with the least amount of resources.

᷿᷿᷿᷿᷿᷿᷿᷿᷿᷿᷿᷿᷿᷿᷿᷿᷿᷿᷿᷿᷿᷿᷿᷿᷿᷿᷿᷿᷿᷿᷿᷿᷿᷿᷿᷿

I have seen countless examples of businesses ignoring the concepts that comprise the Unique Selling Proposition methodology and therefore waste huge amounts of their time, talent, and money on Marketing and Sales programs that would have been much more effective if they had followed the Unique Selling Proposition approach to Marketing and Sales. By properly applying these four steps in defining your Unique Selling Proposition, you will be most effective in scaling the wall surrounding your potential Customers.

᷿᷿᷿᷿᷿᷿᷿᷿᷿᷿᷿᷿᷿᷿᷿᷿᷿᷿᷿᷿᷿᷿᷿᷿᷿᷿᷿᷿᷿᷿᷿᷿᷿᷿᷿᷿᷿

Your communication with your prospect or Customer should be a dialogue, not a monologue; using the Unique Selling Proposition approach can foster that dialogue. A key tool in developing your sales process is to ask questions of your potential Customer so you can fully understand and clarify their goals. Asking open-ended questions can also guide you in exploring the emotional state they want to be in or want to avoid.

In Chapter 5, we discussed developing a profile of your purchaser and decision maker; this is one place where you can very effectively utilize this information. By using the pre-identified profile of your potential buyer, you will have a wealth of insights into how to construct your Unique Selling

Proposition. Another tool to use in developing an effective sales process is to use the phrase "so what" as a transition in your sales message to bring the benefit or attractiveness of your solution to life.

Several years ago I had interesting example of bringing the benefit to life while working with a CPA firm that specialized in auditing. As I discussed their auditing services "product" with the CPA firm's owner and what the benefit of their product was, an interesting dialog developed. He said the benefit of their product was to provide accurate financial statements. So I asked him, "What is the benefit of having accurate financial statements?" He responded, "So you can tell how the business is doing." I responded, "So what? Why is it important to know how the business is doing?" He said, "To determine if you're making a profit or incurring a loss."

I then replied, "Why is it important to know if you're making a profit or loss?" He answered, "To know how the business is impacting your personal finances." I then asked him, "Why is it important to know how the business is impacting your personal finances?" He replied, "Because your personal financial situation will determine whether you'll be able to achieve your goals in life." Finally, I said to him that "achieving your goals in life" is the solution that he is in fact selling. In other words, by having your accounting records properly audited you are providing the assurance that your business will enable you to reach your personal goals in life. Once he understood this, he realized how he needed to bring his auditing services "product" to life at an emotional level with his Customer.

Complete exercise 6-5 in workbook

SALES IS AN ONGOING PROCESS

At the beginning of this section we discussed the importance of having an effective Sales Process. Related to this, I want to emphasize the word "Process"— it is ongoing, not a single event. It is a process with these three aspects:

1. A dialogue leading to a relationship
2. The initial taste of an experience worth repeating
3. Continuous improvement of your Sales Processes

1. A dialogue leading to a relationship

As we discussed above, the Sales Process should be a dialogue with Customers regarding their goals, their desired emotional state, and how your product fulfills their needs—not a monologue of how great your business is or your product's stellar attributes. This dialogue should lead to an ongoing relationship with the sales experience being the beginning of the relationship with you and your business, not the end of it.

2. The initial taste of an experience worth repeating

Your Sales Process should be the start of an experience that your Customer cannot wait to repeat. Back in Chapter 5, we discussed how repeat sales and referrals are developed as a by-product of your business. This experience begins with what your Customer experiences during your Sales Process.

3. Continuous improvement of your Sales Processes

An effective Sales Process is one that has been tested and refined, confirming that it is the optimal sales method for your business—and is the method consistently used by all your personnel. You can develop optimal Sales Processes by requesting input from all your Sales personnel. (I will discuss this more fully in Chapter 9.) It is imperative that everyone uses the *same sales process* and that it is not left up to each sales person to do what works best for her or him. If you leave the Sales Process up to each person, you have no real Sales Process. You will receive less than ideal results, and you will lack the ability to properly oversee your Sales operation.

ʔʔ

One thing you can do to verify that your sales process is being used, used properly, and will validate its effectiveness is to hire people to pose as supposed potential Customers (secret shoppers) in order to test your sales process.

ʔʔ

Part of your Sales Process or sales presentation needs to be a request for the potential Customers to do something. Ideally you ask for an order. However, if that isn't accomplished, you can ask for something else—a commitment to take a specific action, something for them to consider or think about, a referral to someone else, or a contact for you to utilize, all with the bottom line being that there is some action that you are requesting them to take. Their agreeing to do something means the door has been opened so you can reconnect with them regarding what they agreed to do. If you did not obtain a sale in the initial encounter with them, this overt or non-apparent commitment on their behalf sets the stage for the next step in your Sales Process—continuing a dialogue with them.

Another great action to take at the end of the sales presentation is to reconnect with them via an emotion you discovered at the beginning of the conversation that was effective in getting past their wall. This action enables you to solidify that you are only trying to help achieve their goals and their desired emotional state. The objective during the Sales Process, not a Sales Event, is to open the door for an ongoing relationship and to ensure that if your potential Customer is not ready to make a purchase decision, a door is left open for more dialogue when the Customer may be more ready.

Complete exercise 6-6 in workbook

MEETING AND EXCEEDING YOUR CUSTOMER'S EXPECTATIONS

Back in Chapter 5 I listed the five basic actions that need to be completed to have an effective Marketing Program or marketing function. We covered actions one through four in Chapter 5. We will now cover action five. If you recall in Chapter 5 we discussed the fact that the power of branding is that it sets an expectation in your Customer's mind about the experience of buying your product or dealing with your business. Therefore, in your effort to try to meet or exceed your Customer's expectations, one of the most crucial things you must do is to properly set and manage your Customer's expectations. If your Customer's hopes are too high, you will end up disappointing them, they will be unhappy with your product, and you can lose them as a Customer.

Even worse, if you end up greatly disappointing them, they can become an advocate against your business in the marketplace.

222222222222222222222222222222222222222222222

We have all heard the saying about how a person or business can take a lifetime to create a great reputation, but that great reputation can be lost in a moment! However, it is even worse once a person has crossed over the line to be an advocate against your business. You can lose an enormous number of Customers or potential Customers as the result of their negative communication in the marketplace.

222222222222222222222222222222222222222222222

Properly setting and managing your Customer's expectations begins with the previously discussed sphere of developing the Attractiveness of Your Solution. As we discussed in Chapter 5 and we will discuss more in Chapter 7, there is a chicken-and-egg syndrome between your Marketing and Sales area and your Production area; nowhere is that more apparent than in the two sections in Chapter 5 titled, The Attractiveness of Your Solution and Their Awareness of Your Solution. You can't just talk about how good a game you play—you have to actually play a good game!

If you promise more than you consistently deliver, you will set up your Customer for disappointment and lay the groundwork in your business for problems with your Customers. As you will see in Chapter 7, to avoid this you must decipher the proper Production processes so you will be able to consistently meet or exceed your Customers' expectations.

Another area where this "talking a good game" versus "playing a good game" is critical is where your sales personnel overpromise the delivery of certain things to your Customer. Again, without specific Sales Processes in place, each of your salespeople will basically do their own thing. In the heat of the battle during a sales presentation, they may end up overpromising or over-committing. Avoiding the above problem is one the driving needs for having Sales Processes in place.

Related to this are word-of-mouth referrals. If you have an unpaid person with nothing to gain and much to lose who possesses creditability and who becomes an advocate for your business, you have an unbelievably powerful marketing force working for you! However, why do so many businesses experience a lack of referrals? Usually because the product or business has not so exceeded the expectations of the Customer so they are unwilling to take the risk to their reputation and sacrifice of their time to become an advocate for a business.

How do you create an advocate for your business? It begins by creating the most Attractive Solution for your Customer that will in turn knock their socks off. Second, you have to build into your Production process the ability to provide this exact product or Solution day in and day out, without fail, to your Customer. Third, through your Marketing and Sales operations you must set the expectations for your product or business in your Customer's mind high enough to get their business, but not so high that you will not be able to consistently achieve their expectations.

These first three steps will only produce satisfied Customers, not raving advocates for your business. To create raving advocates, you have to set the proper expectations by fully understanding what the Customer really wants and then not only meeting that expectation, but actually and consistently exceeding those expectations!

How do you do that? As you will see in Chapter 7, you accomplish this by understanding from a Production point of view what is the absolutely best product you can provide with one hundred percent consistency to your Customer; then you commit to produce this product. However, you actually provide a better product than you promise by at least one percent because you have pre-engineered more attributes, characteristics, and benefits into the product by building it into your processes. In this way, you will consistently exceed your Customer's expectation! The above is just like the strategy in a war, in that you do not commit all your troops to a battle; you save some as a reserve. Therefore, you do not commit your reserve during the Marketing and Sales processes, but you save it for exceeding your Customer's expectation when you deliver the product, which is your solution to their need.

The trickiest thing about doing this is that the promised expectation must be high enough to garner the sale from you Customer, but low enough that you can exceed it by providing or doing more than the Customer bargained for. This is the essence of the saying "under-promise and over-deliver." This is a complex, delicate balance, and one which we will examine in Chapter 7.

Complete exercise 6-7 in workbook

ASSESSING YOUR COMPETITION

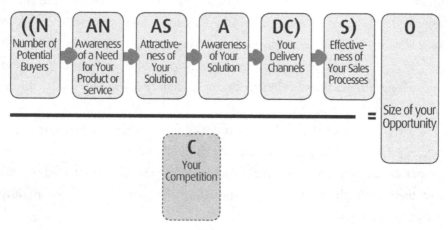

Fig. 6-4

Since it is unlikely that you will control one hundred percent of your market, the last element of your Marketing and Sales area is assessing your competition and planning for how to deal with them. This step includes determining who your competition is, what their strengths and weaknesses are, how much market share you have now, and how much market share you will later possess. Whereas the other six elements of your Marketing and Sales function are offensive in nature, this last one is defensive.

Here's a quick review, using an example to illustrate what we have covered so far with regard to the first six elements of the formula for your Marketing and Sales area:

You have determined that you want to fulfill active women's need for a "high-performance" anti-perspirant, and you have determined the number of potential buyers in your market segment—active women from age 18 to 45 who participate in sports or other performance activities such as acting or dancing.

You have determined that virtually all women in your market segment are aware of a need for a high-performance anti-perspirant.

Your solution for their need will be very attractive because your anti-perspirant will come in various fragrances and serve the multiple purpose of being an anti-perspirant, skin conditioner, and a perfume.

You will be creating an awareness of your perfumed deodorant in your buyer's mind by use of a well-planned and generously funded campaign to give out free samples in newspapers, women's magazines, and via direct mail.

You will use two main delivery channels: retail sales in stores and direct shipments to your Customers who order through the Internet and by use of toll-free numbers.

You have created an effective Sales Process built on all of the above and which uses a Unique Selling Proposition model.

In summary, you have developed a very desirable and comprehensive Marketing and Sales Program and you have defined an enormous market opportunity. In the above, you still have not addressed one final issue: your competition and their products. Unless you can drive them all out of business, you will not control the entire market. Therefore, to realistically account for your portion of your market opportunity, you must divide up the size of your overall opportunity by the number of competitors you have. This leads us to the last element of your comprehensive Marketing and Sales area: the Number of Competitors You Have.

As we discussed at the beginning of this chapter, the formula for the Marketing and Sales area is not a mathematical formula but is instead a conceptual formula. Therefore, you cannot actually calculate the size of your opportunity by just multiplying the previous factors and then dividing that product by the number of competitors you have in order to identify your share of the market. But from a conceptual standpoint, the size of your market is impacted by your competitors. Consequently, you must understand your competitors, how they will respond to you, how they will affect you, and how your business will affect them.

You have to know your competition to beat them.

You will want to collect at least the following general information about each of your main competitors and then perform an analysis of these competitors. Keep in mind that there can be many more factors, some of which are related to the characteristics that were included in the profile of your Customer we discussed back in Chapter 5:

- Revenue
- Profits
- Financial strength
- Number of employees
- Regions served
- Rural or urban areas targeted
- The demographics of their target markets
- Marketing orientation
- Brand strength

Prior to the advent of the Internet, it took a significant amount of effort to obtain the above information. Now, you can develop a fairly complete list of your competitors just by doing an Internet search based on the keywords related to your product. Then you can garner quite detailed information about each of your competitors' businesses and their products just by visiting their web sites.

Once the above analysis of your competitors has been completed, the next step is to develop your knowledge of your competitors' products by obtaining or developing the following detailed information. Be sure to include your direct competitors, indirect competitors, as well as competitors with products that can be substituted for your product (which makes them a competitor to your product). By the way, some business owners think they have no competitors; this is rarely true but even if it were, you would still have some indirect competitors because someone can always substitute another product for your product.

Here is the information you need to collect:

- What is the product name?
- What is the business name?
- What are the strengths and weaknesses of their product?
- What are the strengths and weaknesses of their company?
- What is their reputation in the marketplace?
- Is their market share increasing or decreasing?
- What is their overall marketing plan or strategy?
- What is their pricing strategy?
- What delivery channels do they use?

You also need to consider the following:

- What do you anticipate your competitors will do in response to your marketing efforts?
- Over time, do you think you will have new or different competitors?

Once you have completed your analysis of your competitors, you use the information you gathered in four ways:

1. To validate or if necessary modify your definition of the need you are going to fulfill (i.e., your market opportunity), who your Customer is, and what your target market segment is.
2. To develop or improve the attractiveness of your solution for your target Customer both now and in the future.
3. To expand or modify your delivery channel strategy.
4. If necessary, to modify your Marketing and Sales strategies. The general rule of thumb here is that you do not use a strategy that is in direct competition with your major competitor's successful marketing

strategy, but you target a different market segment or develop a marketing strategy that sets you and your product apart from your competition.

Complete exercise 6-8 in workbook

UPDATING YOUR CRITICAL SUCCESS FACTORS

Back in Chapter 4 you identified the Critical Success Factors for your business. Now that you have completed analyzing your Sales and related area, review and if necessary, modify and/or add to the Critical Success Factors you have already identified.

ZZZZZZZZZZZZZZZZZZZZZZZZZZZZZZZZZZZZZZZZZZZZ

THE SOLUTION

During one-on-one meetings with Sam and meetings we had with his sales staff, Sam realized he needed to build an effective sales process from the ground up based on his unique selling proposition. As a result of this break-though, his business saw a dramatic turnaround. He now understood that the same building blocks that he used in developing his excellent marketing materials could and should be used in developing his sales process.

By understanding that his Customer was a "walled city," he fully developed his business's unique selling proposition. This included identifying the components of his big idea, identifying its big benefit, stating his big promise, and then providing proof of his claims within his sales process. He founded his detailed sales process on the same concept that he used in his marketing material—that his printing business could generate additional revenue for his Customers by presenting a professional image in the printed materials they provided to their Customers.

Sam also realized that a key ingredient of having an effective sales process was to build ongoing "win/win" relationships with his Customers in which he regularly provided value to them even though he may not have made a sale. He did this by changing the sales process to become a consultative experience where the salesperson showed the Customer how they could improve their printed materials and thereby create a better image for their business.

This recognition that sales was an ongoing process enabled him to fully implement the idea of creating "experiences worth repeating" and allowed him to meet and exceed his Customer's expectations, therefore yielding his business additional repeat sales and tremendously increased referrals.

Another key ingredient for Sam in developing an effective sales process was the systematic research that he did on the strengths and weaknesses of his competitors. By incorporating this competitive market information in his sales process, he was able to give his salespeople an edge when they were in the trenches with competitive sales situations.

ZZZZZZZZZZZZZZZZZZZZZZZZZZZZZZZZZZZZZZZZZZZZZZ

STEP #5:
PRODUCING
YOUR PRODUCT
OR SERVICE

ʑʑ

THE CHALLENGE

Peter, a relaxed and easygoing family man in his late forties, faced a huge challenge: to totally remake his construction support business in a very short period of time because of tremendous economic changes buffeting his industry.

As he considered his options, Peter had realized that his product and his employees' skill sets were very applicable to another market. Because of an economic meltdown in his market, he had decided to repurpose all of his business's operations and retrain his staff for a new market. This entailed redirecting his sales and marketing effort toward this different industry as well as changing the product he delivered so it was suitable for this new market. But where would he start and what steps would he need to take to totally remake his business?

ʑʑ

WHAT PRODUCTION MEANS

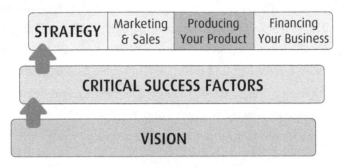

| STRATEGY | Marketing & Sales | Producing Your Product | Financing Your Business |

CRITICAL SUCCESS FACTORS

VISION

Fig. 7-1

Production is the area of your business in which you actually create the product you are providing to your Customer to generate revenue for your business. When I say "Production" most people think "manufacturing;" however, you need to expand your concept of Production because each and every business has a production area.

For instance, if you are restaurant, your Production function would include: choosing the location for your restaurant, creating and decorating your restaurant, maintaining your restaurant, creating the emotional experience you wish Customers to have (i.e., ambience), welcoming them, seating them, taking their orders, procuring, receiving, and storing the food needed, creating new menu items, preparing the food, serving Customers, resolving problems with their orders, charging and collecting payment for their food, obtaining feedback from their experience at your restaurant, and many, many other steps in between.

Production is the core of your business.

Think of your Production area and your Marketing and Sales area like a football game. Your Marketing and Sales area is the process of coming up with the game plan for winning the game; your Production area is actually going out on the field and executing that game plan. As we have said, it is one thing to talk a good game, and it is an entirely different thing to play a good game. If a person talks a good game (I am using "good" as is commonly used in talking about ballgames, but in reality you want your business to be "great" or "excellent" not just "good") but then falls on their face in the actual game, they become a laughingstock to everyone who watched or discussed the game afterwards.

This occurs each year before the annual Super Bowl football game. As the game day draws closer, the hype of what one team will do to the other team becomes louder and louder, and some very big predictions or boasts are made. If in the actual game the team or players making these predictions or boasts fall flat on their faces, then not only are they humiliated but in the future those players' or team's word is doubted since their previous words were not backed up by actions.

These predictions are very similar to the claims made as part of a business's Marketing and Sales efforts. If you make claims that are not consistently fulfilled by your business, then your Customers will doubt your business and its products; at some point, they will no longer be your Customers. And they may tell other potential Customers not to do business with you because you made predictions, boasts, and claims in your Marketing and Sales that you did not fulfill. As we said above, it is one thing to talk a good game and it is an entirely different thing to play a good game. So your Production area includes the entire realm of playing a good game, thus enabling you to produce revenue for your business.

ʔʔʔ

EQUIPMENT VS. TOOLS

There are some terms and processes used in this chapter with regard to a "manufacturing" environment for producing a product. Two of these terms are "equipment" and "tools." In this chapter and the remaining chapters, I use these terms in a generic sense, not a literal sense. For instance, "equipment" may be used to connote a personal computer, and "tool" may be used to indicate an electronic spreadsheet for a personal computer. So "equipment" and "tools" or other terms that generally apply to a "manufacturing" environment should all be viewed as something that is of assistance to you in producing your product.

ʔʔ

THE PRODUCTION CHICKEN-AND-EGG SYNDROME

So we see that there is a close interrelationship between your Production area and your Marketing and Sales area. One thing that must be fully recognized and completely understood is that there is a chicken-and-egg syndrome between your Production area and your Marketing and Sales area as well. The Structure of Profitability™ diagram in Chapter 2 shows that your Marketing and Sales area leads to your Production area. In Chapter 5, we looked at your Solution to the market opportunity that presents itself to you, and we discussed the process for determining and fully developing the Attractiveness of your Solution in light of the opportunity that is presented to you via your target market. Here is the formula that we discussed in Chapter 5 for determining Attractiveness of Your Solution in your Marketing and Sales area:

Fig. 7-2

So where does the chicken-and-egg syndrome come into play? How do you know what you can bring to the marketplace with regard to the Attractiveness of Your Solution (talking a good game) without first working on your Production area to determine how you plan to follow through and actually play a good game? What's more, are you positive that can you execute your game plan? Or will you miss the mark and disappoint your Customers?

Hence the chicken-and-egg syndrome is that while your Marketing and Sales area leads to your Production area (how you are going to produce what you are marketing and selling), it is your expertise in your Production area that drives your Marketing and Sales area. Specifically, to some degree you must figure out how you will meet your potential Customer's expectations you are creating in their mind (which you do in your Production area) before you engage in the effort to create these expectations via your Marketing and Sales area.

There is no perfect solution to this dilemma; the best outcome is that you make three separate evaluations of your Production area. The first analysis should be part of the "conceptualizing what your business is all about" process (discussed in Chapter 3) you perform while you are developing your Vision for your business. This initial analysis is where you construct the overall game plan for delivering the "win" to your Customer. This first step would be like deciding if you should even join the league in order to play with the other teams; that is, can you realistically compete with the other teams (your competitors) in this league?

The second analysis of your Production area involves reviewing your resources and your Production capabilities so you can figure out a preliminary game plan. The result of this second analysis is a general and overall game plan of how you will meet the expectations (in your Production area) of your Customer you are creating in your potential Customer's mind (Marketing and Sales) before you engage in the effort to actually create these expectations. This is exactly what we did back in Chapter 5 when we looked at the above formula to determine and develop the Attractiveness of Your Solution.

In this chapter, we will perform a third analysis at a much deeper level, and we will closely examine how to actually produce the results (i.e., the execution of a detailed game plan).

OVERVIEW OF YOUR PRODUCTION AREA

The formula for actually producing the product(s) that you are going to sell to your Customer is the following:

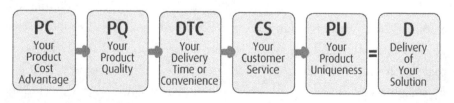

Fig. 7-3

For your business to appraise its competitive advantage, as well as lay out its overall game plan and assess its Production capabilities, you must determine the relative strengths and weaknesses of producing and delivering the product (your solution) you have developed to fulfill a need in the marketplace. The above formula leads you through this assessment. Listed below is a short explanation of each element of the Production area formula:

Delivery of Your Solution—The product of this formula, or the overarching question is: How are you going to provide your solution? The desirability of the actual creation and delivery of your solution is determined by the factors, explained below, shown at the right of the equation.

Your Product Cost Advantage —Is your business consistently able to produce your product at a lower cost than your competition?

The Quality of Your Product—Is the quality of your product consistently higher in obvious ways than your competitor's product quality?

Your Delivery Time or Convenience—Do you deliver or provide your product sooner or more quickly than your competition? Or are you more convenient to your Customer than your competition?

Your Customer Service—Is your Customer service reliably better than your competition's Customer services?

The Uniqueness of Your Product—Does your product possess some desirable unique trait(s) that your competition cannot duplicate or obtain because of some impediment (e.g., a patent, copyright, trade secret, extreme cost to develop, etc.)?

Let's apply the above formula to an example. If all five of the production factors are strengths for your business—you are the low-cost producer of your product, your product quality is greater than your competition, your delivery time or convenience is better than your competitors, your Customer service is better than your competitors, and your product is totally unique—then you would have complete dominance of your target market.

So, this formula serves four incredible purposes in your business:

1. It can be used as a *market analysis tool* for you to analyze the market for any one of your existing products or to analyze a market that you

are contemplating entering. In this case, you would utilize this tool to evaluate and categorize the strengths and weaknesses of the existing products in the market and thereby evaluate your opportunities for entering the new market.

2. The formula can be used as a *competitive analysis assessment tool* to evaluate how your business is doing in providing a desirable and differentiated product to your current marketplace. Using the formula in this second way allows you to score your business on how well it is executing and provides you with insights to understand how each of your products is actually operating.

3. The formula can serve as a *planning tool* to guide and show you specifically what things you can to do to improve your performance. To obtain an accurate, realistic, and specific appraisal of what you need to do to enhance your operations, this planning exercise needs to be performed along with the above competitive analysis assessment step at the individual product level, not globally for your entire business. Thereafter, you would assess your business's ability to provide a better or improved product to the marketplace.

4. The formula can operate as a *resource allocation evaluation tool* to ensure that your business is executing properly and allocating its resources properly in the areas that will separate your business and its product from your competition. This evaluation tool serves as a yardstick or indicator you can use to determine if you are doing what you need to do today and plan on doing in the future to be fully successful. The outcome from this planning exercise will be guidance on what areas of your business you want to focus.

THE FIVE ELEMENTS OF YOUR STRATEGIC ADVANTAGE

We will be examining in detail each of these five elements of your Production function to show you how to assess the strengths and weaknesses of your business in each area. However, I would like to alert you to the fact that as we proceed through this analysis, it is vitally important that you ask yourself, "Which of these five areas is the key to my Production area?" When I say "key to your Production area" I mean what is the one thing that, from a Production standpoint, separates you from your competitors? I call this your Strategic Advantage. Furthermore, once you have discerned your Strategic Advantage, it should be the basis for developing the Attractiveness of your Solution in your Marketing and Sales area.

This entire chapter will provide you with the tools you will need to figure out your Strategic Advantage and integrate that into your business so you can provide your Strategic Advantage to your Customers on an unfailing basis. Since this feature (or a combination of factors) separates you from your competitors, you will want to make your Strategic Advantage the foundation of developing the Attractiveness of your Solution in your Marketing and Sales area. I will elaborate on the concept of your Strategic Advantage later in this chapter.

There are three ways of proceeding with your analysis of the Production area of your business:

1. Perform the following analysis separately for each of your products. By using this approach you will have much more detailed information regarding your Production area; however, much of it may be redundant since the information you could obtain may apply to your other products as well.
2. Perform this analysis by using the same overall target markets that you defined in your Marketing and Sales area.
3. Combine all your target markets for all your products and perform a combined analysis of all of these markets and products in one gigantic sweep.

My recommendation is that if your business has relatively few products which are targeted at one or several markets and the markets are fairly similar, use option three; combine all your target markets for all your products and perform one combined analysis. Of course, where you have indications that the results for a specific product or target market differ from your other products or target markets, then you would need to perform a separate analysis.

If your business has a significant number of products that are targeted at one or more similar markets, or if you have relatively few products but they are targeted at several dissimilar markets, then I would use option two and perform this analysis separately for each target market. Option one, which involves the most work, should be used when you have a large number of products and they are targeted at a number of dissimilar markets; in that case, your research and analysis would have little redundancies.

EXCEPTIONAL VERSUS GREAT VERSUS GOOD VERSUS AVERAGE

Many business owners have told me, "I want to provide exceptional product quality and exceptional customer service, and exceptional…" While it may be admirable and desirable to provide an exceptionally low price, or exceptional product quality, or exceptional delivery time or convenience, or exceptional customer service, or an exceptional product by having a totally unique product, being exceptional just does not happen by wishing so and saying you are exceptional! There are various levels that a business can target in each of the above five Production areas. I use the following scale to evaluate the various areas of a business: poor, average, good, great, and excellent.

One of the most crucial things to realize regarding your business's relative performance is that it costs more and takes more effort for your company to be good rather than average in a certain area. It costs still more and takes much more effort for your company to be great rather than good in a certain area. Lastly, it costs a very large amount more and takes much, much more effort for your company to be excellent rather than great in a certain area. As a business owner, this means you have to realize moving your business from one level to the next higher level does not just happen (this also includes moving from poor to average) but requires concentrated effort, more work, new processes, and additional costs on your behalf. To move up to a higher level on your cost advantage, the quality of your Product, your delivery time or convenience, your customer service, or the uniqueness of your Product, you must dedicate your entire focus and resources.

Let us pretend that your business is an airline and you want to improve the quality of the service your flight attendants provide. Most likely to do this you would have to hire more flight attendants, provide more training, implement better and more Customer-focused processes, upgrade their uniforms, improve the ambience of the inside of your airplanes, provide additional services—all of which almost assuredly will cost more than you were spending before.

Having worked with numerous businesses, I have found that generally as you continue up the scale of moving your business or product from poor to average, average to good, good to great, and great to excellent, each successive step costs more and requires more effort to accomplish. The important thing to recognize is that most likely it will cost you more for each step compared to the costs of the prior step to move up the ladder from average to good, from good to great and from great to excellent.

Furthermore, to improve any of the five areas of your Production area you cannot just say, "We will try harder" or "We will do better" and have your business and your employees respond to the challenge and summon all their energy and intestinal fortitude to produce better results. The "we try harder" approach may work for a short period of time and, just like an athlete, you may be able to rise above yourself and take it to a higher gear, but unless you have made systematic changes to your business and its processes, after a period of time your performance will return to what it was before.

Consequently there are three import steps that must be very clearly kept in mind:

1. A cost benefit analysis should be performed to determine if the benefits you will obtain from making the changes are greater than your costs.
2. The decision to improve a certain area should be viewed as a strategic decision driven by input from your Marketing and Sales area so you can understand how making the change will impact how the Attractiveness of Your Solution is perceived by your target market. The entire decision to try to improve any element of your Production area should be done in concert with input from your Marketing and Sales area so you do not spend time and money on

something that may have a marginal or no impact on your projected revenues.

3. As was discussed above, to obtain sustainable results from your changes, you must systematize the changes so you are able to produce the desired result on a consistent basis. I will discuss the systematization of all the aspects of your business further in Chapter 9.

Bear in mind in this discussion that for most businesses, being excellent in a large number of areas is not practical—but that does not mean that you are letting an area or function go to pot. Quite the contrary, having a function that is good or an area that is great does not just accidentally occur; it is a result of having systems in place, providing the proper training, focused attention, and by rewarding innovation. It is important to realize that you do not have unlimited resources, and that you must allocate your resources of time, money, and talent in the areas of your business that you think will provide you the most incremental value. Always remember that if you neglect an area and do not allocate the proper resources to that area or function, its performance or results could drop to poor or worse over time.

PRODUCT COST ADVANTAGE

Fig. 7-4

As you examine your Production area, determine whether you have an advantage or a disadvantage with regard to the cost of producing your products compared to your competitors. If your production costs are lower, then you have a cost advantage; however, if your production costs are higher than your competitors, then you have a cost disadvantage.

Why is this important? This question is vitally important because if you will review the formula for the Attractiveness of Your Solution, you will see that the first element is your Price Advantage and having a price advantage means you actually sell your product at a lower price than your competitors. For your business to have a sustainable Price Advantage, you must first have a Product Cost Advantage, because unless you do, all you are going to get by selling your product at a price lower than your competitors is to lower your profits and perhaps put your business at risk, which might in turn cause your business to fail!

There are two timeframes with regard to having a Product Cost Advantage or disadvantage. The first is having a Product Cost Advantage or disadvantage at the present time. The second timeframe is your hope of having a Product Cost Advantage in the future. As the saying goes, a bird in hand is better than two in the bush; it is the same with your hope for and plans for having a Product Cost Advantage in the future. If you base some or all of your Attractiveness of Your Solution on your Price Advantage, but your hoped-for Product Cost Advantage does not become a reality in the future, then you have a major problem—you will have to either raise your prices or accept the long-term prospect of lower profits for your business.

Having higher profits from the sale of your product is always desirable, but certain industries are somewhat constrained in their ability to raise prices to obtain additional profits. For these types of industries, increasing your profits by having lower production costs is fundamental. These businesses are in fact driven by having lower costs, which therefore makes this a key element for them. Some of these types of businesses are commodities (corn, sugar, gold, e.g.), retail, industries in which products are considered a commodity (i.e., commercial rolls of toilet paper) because it is difficult to differentiate your product from your competitors' product.

Of course, product cost as it relates to your sales price determines your level of profit from a sales transaction; however, as we discussed back in Chapter 5, if your market is price-sensitive, then producing your product at a lower cost becomes even more significant because your selling price may be constrained.

Complete exercise 7-1 in workbook

PRODUCT QUALITY

Fig. 7-5

Next, as you consider your Production area, you want to ascertain whether you have a strength or weakness with regard to the quality of your product compared to your competition. This is the most straightforward element of your Production area, and it lends itself to independent verification of your perception of quality. The most common mistake made with regard to the Quality of Your Product is that you assume your perception of quality is the same as your Customers' or your target market's assessment of your the Quality of Your Product.

There are three ways to assess the Quality of Your Product. The first method is a subjective analysis based on your sales volume and the input from your sales personnel. The second method is to use independent surveys to objectively analyze your current Customers' perception of the Quality of Your Product. The third method is to have an independent consumer research and testing lab such Consumer Reports® or JD Power and Associates® analyze your product compared to competing products. With regard to survey results and independent testing findings, keep in mind that if your target Customers' perception of the Quality of Your Product significantly differs from the true and actual Quality of Your Product, then you may have a problem in your Marketing and Sales area that needs to be addressed.

ꝚꝚꝚꝚꝚꝚꝚꝚꝚꝚꝚꝚꝚꝚꝚꝚꝚꝚꝚꝚꝚꝚꝚꝚꝚꝚꝚꝚꝚꝚꝚꝚꝚꝚꝚꝚꝚꝚꝚ

MARKET QUALITY

One may immediately assume that if the quality of your product is higher than your competitors' then you have a quality advantage. However, if you are not using this quality advantage as a marketing benefit, then you may be incurring additional costs to produce a higher quality product, but the quality advantage of your product is not translating to additional sales. Once again, this is why a synergistic or symbiotic relationship between your Marketing and Sales area and your Production area exists and must be recognized. Take a holistic approach to developing and operating the Marketing and Sales and Production areas of your business so you can take full advantage of all the attributes of your product and/or business.

ʔʔ

Just like in the above Product Cost Advantage section, here are two timeframes with regard to having a Quality advantage or disadvantage. The first timeframe is having a Quality advantage or disadvantage at the present time and the second is your hope of having a Quality advantage in the future. Once again, if you base some or all of your Attractiveness of Your Solution on your Quality advantage, and your Quality does not become a reality in the future, then you have a major problem because you will be talking a good game but not playing a good game.

Having a higher quality Product compared to your competition is very desirable, especially in three industries that are particularly driven by higher quality products (making this a key element)—jewelry, automobiles, and clothing.

Complete exercise 7-2 in workbook

DELIVERY TIME OR CONVENIENCE

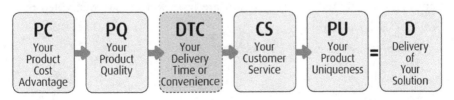

Fig. 7-6

The third element of your Production area involves whether or not you deliver or provide your Product sooner or more quickly than your competition or that dealing with you is more convenient to your Customer than dealing with your competition. Establish whether you have an advantage or a disadvantage with regard to the period of time it takes from the point an order is placed with your business to the point at which you deliver your product to your Customer. Additionally, you need to evaluate whether you have an advantage or a disadvantage when it comes to how convenient it is for your Customer to transact business with you compared to doing business with your competition.

The issue of convenience shows up in two ways. First, if your Customer comes to your physical location, how convenient is your location to physically get to or if you go to their location, how convenient is it to get to your Customer from your location? Second, if your business provides its product from a remote location and your Customer only interacts with your business via a web site or a telephone number (and therefore they do not have to go to your physical location), how convenient and easy to use is your web site or telephone operation? Keep in mind that if you operate from a remote location, your Product quality does not include the quality of your Customer's shopping experience in obtaining the product from you. The quality of their shopping experience falls into your Delivery Time or Convenience area because it involves how convenient and therefore how pleasurable your Customer's shopping experience was.

Delivering or providing your Product sooner or more quickly than your competition or being more convenient are advantageous attributes for every business. But the three industries that are especially driven by delivery time or convenience, making it a key element, are fast food restaurants, video rental locations, and gas stations.

Complete exercise 7-3 in workbook

CUSTOMER SERVICE

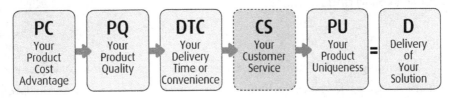

Fig. 7-7

Fourthly, as you analyze your Customer Service area, you want to verify whether you have a strength or weakness with regard to the Customer Service that a Customer or potential Customer experiences when they interact with you compared to interacting with your competitor. Sometimes it is difficult to define what is and what is not included as part of a business's Customer Service. This is particularly true when your business is a distribution, wholesale, or retail business. Then the concept of Customer Service becomes somewhat fuzzy. Essentially, Customer Service is the overall experience a Customer has in dealing with you, which includes the entire shopping experience they have with your business.

Customer Service includes all the interactions that a Customer or potential Customer has with your business to obtain your product. Customer Service does not include your actual product or the price of that product, but it does include placing an order, inquiring about resolving an order or product issue before the delivery of your product, post product-delivery issues, and problem resolution once your product has been received by your Customer. Let me underscore: Resolution of problems or concerns with your Product or issues involving your Customer's shopping experience fall squarely within your Customer Service function.

ʓʓ

CUSTOMER SERVICE VERSUS MARKETING

It should be noted that the term "Customer Service" infers that you are not a Customer until you make a purchase, which means that prior to becoming a Customer, interactions with your target audience fall within your Marketing and Sales area.

zzzzzzzzzzzzzzzzzzzzzzzzzzzzzzzzzzzzzzzzzzzzzzzz

Depending on the business, a Customer Service function may include operations that take place in your Marketing and Sales area (i.e., the pre- and post-sales service that your potential Customer receives from your sales personnel) and your Finance and Administration area (e.g., resolving invoice problems, handling of returned products). It should be noted that from an overall standpoint, Customer Service is the experience that a Customer has in dealing with you as a business but not their experience with your actual product.

Once again, there are two timeframes to having a Customer Service advantage or disadvantage—the present time and in the future. If you base some or all of the Attractiveness of Your Solution on your Customer Service advantage, and your Customer Service is lacking now, and if it does not become an advantage in the future, then you have a major problem because you will be talking a good game, but not backing up your talk by playing a good game. One method you can use to verify that your Customer Service function is operating correctly is to hire people to purchase your product and then give feedback on the purchasing process. Alternatively, you or one of your staff can make phone calls to various Customers to check in with them to see how your business is doing in meeting their expectations (lack of meeting your Customer's expectations also includes your Customer Service operation).

While having a Customer Service advantage over your competitors is always very desirable, there are certain industries where having better Customer Service is imperative: insurance, accounting services, and pharmacies. Within these business sectors, Customers perceive each business's products to be almost identical or involve situations where they really do not have the knowledge to differentiate between the various products of competing businesses.

Complete exercise 7-4 in workbook

THE UNIQUENESS OF YOUR PRODUCT

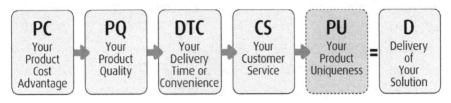

Fig. 7-8

Lastly, in the Delivery of Your Solution, you should scrutinize your Product to determine whether you have any desirable unique characteristics or features. The Uniqueness of Your Product is not something that simply happens; you must create or develop this uniqueness. While it originates from your Production area, the benefit is obtained in the Marketing and Sales area because you are able to deliver a Uniquely Attractive Solution to your Customer's needs, which should generate additional revenue for your business.

As we discussed previously, because your product possesses some desirable unique trait and your competition cannot duplicate or obtain this desirable unique trait due to some impediment (e.g., a patent, a copyright, a trade secret, or extreme cost to develop), you are able to sell your product at a higher price than your competition, and you do not have to focus on your Product Quality, Delivery Time or Convenience, and Customer Service areas as much because you are the only game in town. All these factors can yield higher than normal profits for your business.

There are three ways in which your business can obtain a product with a unique feature or a totally unique product:

1. Purchase the rights for the product from someone else.
2. Create the unique feature or a totally unique product as a byproduct of your normal Production process.
3. Create the unique feature or a totally unique product as an intentional step in a Research and Development area.

The third approach may be the most expensive way of creating a unique product; however, it may be a necessary cost so your business can maintain its competitive advantage.

When you observe each of the formulas for the three areas of your business that were discussed in Chapter 2, you will not see an area titled Research and Development because it is contained inside the Production area as the development arm of The Uniqueness of Your Product area. In reality, your Research and Development function may be housed in a different building than your Production function or even in a different city, state, or country. From a strategic point of view, the purpose of your Research and Development function is to enable the Delivery of Your Solution to be more effective.

In my opinion, in a correctly structured business, your Research and Development function operates as a joint venture between your Marketing and Sales area and your Production area. Your Research and Development function may be driven either by the personnel in your Marketing and Sales area and/or your Research and Development personnel. No matter who is the driving force for your Research and Development function, Marketing and Sales area personnel need to be involved at a certain point so all the factors that determine the Size of Your Opportunity can be assessed and fully developed to ascertain the commercial viability of the newly created product.

While having a unique product always provides you with an advantage over your competition, there are certain industries in which having a unique product creates an enormous advantage for a business. Industries where The Uniqueness of Your Product can provide a massive advantage are health care, computer hardware and software, and manufacturing.

Complete exercise 7-5 in workbook

DEVELOPING YOUR STRATEGIC ADVANTAGE

Once you have examined each of the five elements of your Production area in detail and assessed their strengths and weaknesses, you should ask yourself which of these five areas is the "key" to your Production area. Think of it as being the one thing that, from a Production standpoint, separates you from your competitors and that, therefore, you will make the foundation of your entire business! There is a saying that "there is wisdom in crowds, but genius in individuals." This can be applied to discovering the key to your Production area. Specifically, your business will remain just part of the crowd of competitors unless you develop your Strategic Advantage, which will then enable you to stand out from the crowd.

Please review the five elements of your Production area and write down which of these elements is the key to your entire business. In certain situations, your key element can also be a combination of two of the elements. For example, "We will produce a high-quality product that is unique," or "We will produce a low-cost, high-quality product" (which translates to a value approach); however, the key to your Production area should rarely include more than two of the elements of your Production area.

As I mentioned in this chapter, I call this one thing that separates you from your competitors your Strategic Advantage. Now that you have discerned your Strategic Advantage, you want to make sure it is the basis of developing the Attractiveness of your Solution in your Marketing and Sales area. Your next step is to return to your Marketing and Sales area and fully develop Your Solution based on your Strategic Advantage from your Production area. This involves reviewing the Attractiveness of Your Solution formula back in Chapter 5 and determining how to utilize your Strategic Advantage as the foundation for the development of the Attractiveness of Your Solution. Bear in mind as you do this, if your Strategic Advantage is being a low-cost producer of your product, then in the Marketing and Sales area, a low-cost producer equates to having a Price Advantage.

Earlier in this chapter we discussed the chicken-and-egg syndrome between your Marketing and Sales area and your Production area. At this point it becomes more obvious that to provide something that meets your Customer's needs in a special way (Your Solution), you must first ascertain how your business will go about producing Your Solution by using your Strategic Advantage as the delineator in your Production. By using it in this way, your Strategic Advantage will set you apart from your competition. An absolute key in this process is that for an element to be your Strategic Advantage, you must deliver it one hundred percent of the time to your Customer. Your Strategic

Advantage must be designed into your Production area, and it must be the bedrock of how you operate your Production area!

To go back to the "talking a good game" versus "playing a good game" analogy, your Strategic Advantage (that which you build into your business from the ground up and that you deliver one hundred percent of the time) is playing a good game. Talking a good game, which is based on your Strategic Advantage, is the development of what you communicate to your potential Customer as part of conveying the Attractiveness of Your Solution, an integral part of your Marketing effort.

Complete exercise 7-6 in workbook

UPDATING YOUR CRITICAL SUCCESS FACTORS

zzzzzzzzzzzzzzzzzzzzzzzzzzzzzzzzzzzzzzzzzzzzzzzzz

THE SOLUTION

As Peter moved forward with the process of redesigning and re-engineering his business, he realized that he was presented with a chicken-and-egg syndrome. Before he could market to this new industry he needed to develop the skill sets and the product for it. However, to truly do that, he needed to get Customers in this new market. Part of this challenge was to perfect his product and its delivery as quickly as possible because of the economic situation. So this is the game plan that we mapped out to solve the dilemma he faced.

First, as well as he could as an outsider, he developed a test product for this new market and retrained a small amount of his staff to have the skill sets needed. Next, he landed a few jobs in this industry by being a low bidder, basically buying the jobs with the lowest price. These actions would give him the "laboratory" to perfect his product so he could both talk a good game (his Marketing and Sales area) and play a good game (his Production area).

As he considered the five elements that we discussed that comprised his Production area, he realized his Strategic Advantage was that he provided an exceptionally high-quality product that was delivered with superior Customer Service. Therefore, he focused his business's energy on fully developing the highest-quality Product and best Customer Service he could provide to this new industry.

Once he proved himself with the initial orders, his reputation began to grow. As quickly as possible, he developed large-scale processes to move his personnel and his production resources to the new market. As his revenue increased, he spent time further expanding his Strategic Advantage for the new industry by developing a still higher-quality product while providing better and better Customer service. Within a short period time, he had become an industry leader in his new market.

ƧƧ

STEP #6: FINANCING YOUR BUSINESS

ꝛꝛ

THE CHALLENGE

Karen, who was a grandmother in her early sixties, was truly excited about her new opportunity. She had been an executive in various home health organizations over the last twenty years, and now she was starting her own home health company. She knew the business backwards and forwards, but only from an operational standpoint. She was a former RN who loved building an organization and its commensurate people to provide high-quality home health care to their patients. While she was looking forward to starting and growing her new business, she was very unsure of the entire financial area of her business, how to plan for the future, and how to track her ongoing performance.

ꝛꝛ

WHY THE FUNDING OF A BUSINESS IS SO IMPORTANT

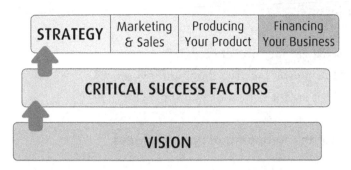

Fig. 8-1

The financing of your business is crucially important to your business's survival and growth. This entire chapter examines how you provide the initial and subsequent financing for your business. The goal of this financing is to construct the organization so it will execute your Strategy, which will in turn enable you to achieve your Vision for your business.

Besides start-up funding, to create a thriving business you are most likely going to require additional funding for your business. Financing a business and planning for its future financial needs can be very daunting areas that have perplexed many business owners. You will find entire books devoted to this many-faceted subject; we cannot possibly delve into all the various issues involving financing in just one chapter. However, I want to provide you with the basic resources and tools with which to navigate this area and help you closely monitor your needs, know when action is required, and determine what measures you should take.

Let's quickly review where we are. You have defined where you want to take your business (your Vision, Critical Success Factors, and Strategy), how you are going to market and sell your Product (your Marketing and Sales area), and how you going to produce what you are marketing and selling (your Production area). While these three areas are the core of your business, the funding and financing area of your business enable, support, and foster the operations of these three core areas.

Here are the three basic concepts you need to review about financing of your business:

1. What are your overall needs?
2. How do you calculate the amount you need?
3. What are the basic sources of financing?

Formula for the financing of your business

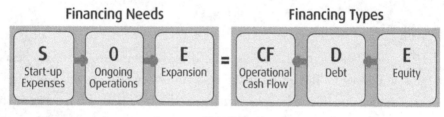

Fig. 8-2

In the above formula, you can see that your need for financing is determined by the costs to start your business (if you are in the start-up mode), your current and ongoing operations, and the costs to expand your business. To meet these needs you have three sources:

1. The cash flow provided by your business's ongoing operations.
2. Debt your business could incur.
3. Equity capital that can be put into your business by an owner.

Unlike the prior chapters where we were able to look at each element of your Marketing and Sales area formula and your Production area formula separately, the elements of the above formula apply to many aspects of the financing of your business. Therefore, I will not cover this information on an element-by-element basis, but rather how the financing of your business applies to the following topics:

- Defining your overall needs for financing?

- Evaluating your financing needs
- Tools for calculating the amount of your financing needs
- Types of financing
- Sources of financing
- Evaluating financing criteria
- The process of obtaining funding

YOUR OVERALL FINANCING NEEDS

There are three basic origins for the financing needs of your business:

1. Start-up expenses of your business
2. Ongoing operations
3. Expansion of your business

Start-up expenses of your business

The start-up expenses include the initial purchase price of your business plus the amount needed for equipment, furniture, other assets, decorating, supplies, utility deposits, down payments, costs to hire and train personnel, initial working capital, and other start-up expenses necessary to begin operation of your business.

Ongoing operations

Ongoing operations have two fundamental areas:

- Seasonal working capital—funds needed only for a certain period of time (less than one year) to finance the accounts receivable, inventory, advances, vehicles, equipment, and furniture and other assets or expenses of your business.
- Permanent working capital—funds needed for at least one year, perhaps forever, to finance the above.

Expansion of your business

- Additional equipment required to expand your business

- Funds to acquire other assets such as furniture, vehicles, or outfitting costs required to expand your business
- Additional utility deposits required to expand your business
- Increased working capital needed to expand your business
- Funds required to expand your research and development expenditures
- Funds required to acquire real estate you may use to expand your business

EVALUATING YOUR FINANCING NEEDS

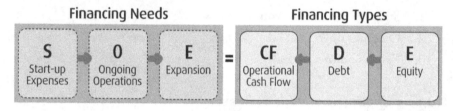

Fig. 8-3

Now that you have an understanding of the general need for financing your business and the scope of your possible needs for financing, the next step is to evaluate your financing needs in those three areas of origin mentioned above:

- Initial start-up expenses of your business
- Ongoing operations
- Expansion of your business model

The goal here is to gain an understanding of the factors and forces that influence and determine your need for financing so you will have a conceptual knowledge of the matters that must be considered first before you attempt to actually calculate your need for financing.

ꝣꝣꝣ

CASH IS KING

Keep in mind that all businesses that fail, fail because they eventually run out of cash. You want to accurately assess and then calculate your available cash and your related need for financing.

ꝣꝣ

As you try to predict your future cash needs, you must first identify the assumptions you will use for forecasting your business's funding requirements. To do this, you should create a list of assumptions and suppositions you are using about the overall operating environment of your business. These assumptions should include factors both inside and external to your business. Write down the foundational support for each assumption so that everyone who will review or utilize the projections can understand and evaluate your assumptions.

Initial start-up expenses of your business

If you have a new business, assessing your start-up expense needs is fairly straightforward. Remember, your start-up financing needs to include not only the funds you will require to purchase assets, set up your place of business, and hire and train personnel, but also will include working capital in case you incur a loss during your start-up phase. The expenses for most start-up businesses will be greater than its revenue; you will have some need for working capital—the initial funding you will require to continue to operate during your start-up period.

Ongoing operations

There are three basic ingredients that will determine the amount of financing you will require for current operations of your business.

1. How profitable is your business? The degree to which a business's revenue is greater than its expenses determines its ability to self-fund its operations and its possible expansion.

2. How quickly are your assets growing? If your assets are growing faster than your profits, there may be a cash-flow crisis looming.

    Note: These first two factors relate to each other because if the growth of your assets is under control, then the more profitable your business is and the smaller will be your need for financing—and it may be that you have no need for financing. From a theoretical standpoint, the more profitable a business is, the more likely it may be able to finance its own growth.

3. How much money are you taking out of the business for you personally? The less money you take out of the business—compensation, fringe benefits, and owner's business expenses—the less money you will need to obtain for your business. We will examine these three areas in more detail in the next section.

Expansion of your business

Getting additional capital for expanding your business is complex. There are two basic financing needs for a business that is trying to scale up its operations to grow and expand: 1) additional assets in the form of equipment, furniture, and related needs, 2) additional working capital in the form of accounts receivable, inventory, equipment, and other needs (miscellaneous receivables, advances, prepaid expenses, etc.).

The same three factors and the related issues that determine your need for financing your ongoing operations also shape your need for funding the expansion of your business. If it is sufficiently profitable, you may be able to fund your expansion out of the cash flow generated by your ongoing operations. If your non-cash assets are growing more slowly than your profits, then you have less money tied in your accounts receivable, inventory, and equipment. As your business grows, the need for outside funding will be smaller.

However, if the cash being generated by additional sales is falling as a percentage of revenue compared to the cash generated previously from sales, that means your profitability is declining. Therefore, unless you decrease the percentage of profits you are taking out of your business, you will either need to add to the equity of your business or increase your debt. Greater debt may take the form of increased Accounts Payable, more current liabilities, or higher long-term debt. Of course, if you are taking additional funds out of the business, these funds aren't available to support growth.

In your effort to grow your business, be aware that expansion involves a big hidden financial risk because growth and expansion can cause cash-flow problems. Many business owners mistakenly think that expansion and growth will produce positive cash flow. While this is a hoped-for situation, it could produce negative cash flow for two reasons: 1) Unless you are very careful, the capital expenditures required for your expansion and any related increase in your working capital needs (accounts receivable, inventory) could be greater than the additional cash generated from the expansion. That is why it is so very important to monitor the growth of your assets. 2) When a business has not adequately engineered the ability to scale their business into their current operations through the use of proper processes and systems, often the result is that the cost of sales and overhead expenses proportionately increase as an unfortunate consequence of the expansion. This results in the business's overall profit margin (business profits divided by gross revenue) falling from its previous benchmark. This means the business is not generating the same percentage of profit from the additional revenue compared to the profit percentage that was generated from the previous revenue.

The consequence of not sustaining your pre-expansion profit margin after the expansion is that the cash-flow assumptions that were used for your projections are not realized. Therefore, the cash generated from your operations is less than anticipated as a result of not properly managing your profit margins in your post-expansion arena. This scenario occurs because with a larger and more complex business, there are more situations the business owner needs to monitor. Unless the business has been properly systematized, the additional complexity from the expansion results in a business that is not managed and operating as well after the expansion as it was before the expansion.

When both of the above occur, a business can end up with cash-flow difficulties, which could be a recipe for disaster. A third ingredient that sometimes contributes to this witch's brew is when the business owner has projected an increase in cash flow as a result of the expansion. They assume that the additional cash is present, and accordingly they take more cash out of the business than they were taking out before. Consequently, you as a business owner need to be very careful about how much cash you take out of the business by closely monitoring your current cash balance and future cash requirements.

I am not at all suggesting you do not pay yourself; however, you should be very careful regarding how much cash you take out so you do not increase your financing needs to an unsustainable amount.

ꝛꝛ

CASH CONSERVATION

If your business is in start-up mode (the first three years of a business), unless your business is extremely profitable, I recommend that to conserve cash for your business's operations and growth you do not take out much money for yourself. After your business is up and running, is viable and financially healthy, then you can increase the amount you transfer from the business to yourself.

ꝛꝛ

Complete exercise 8-1 in workbook

TOOLS FOR CALCULATING YOUR FINANCING NEEDS

There are four primary tools that can be used to specifically determine the amount of funding your business will require.

Start-up expense checklist

Calculating your initial funding needs for starting a business is relatively straightforward because basically all you have to do is determine what you need to begin operating, the specific amounts for each need, then total them. Please see Fig. 8-4 on the following page for the checklist.

Complete exercise 8-2 in workbook

There are many financing/financial analysis tools. In this book, we are solely talking about the financing of a business, so I have chosen to limit the discussion to the following three essential financial tools.

Monthly and annual budgets

The use of monthly and annual budgets can provide you with the information you will require to forecast your financing needs. Creating monthly and annual budgets is fairly straightforward; however, here are a few things to keep in mind:

- Ensure that you create a budget line item for each of the possible revenue, expense, asset, or liability categories you will incur. Make sure you budget for both monthly items and non-monthly items. It is easy to recall monthly expenditures and easy to overlook non-monthly expenditures like quarterly vehicle insurance payments, semi-annual real estate taxes, or repairs and maintenance that occur irregularly throughout the year. Do three budget projections—a high, low, and "most likely" scenario. Use the best- and worst-case budget projections to develop contingency plans that would be employed if these two alternative situations presented themselves.
- Compare your actual financial statement results to your budget amounts to analyze the differences between the figures and take corrective actions if required.

Complete exercise 8-3 in workbook

Item	Monthly Amount	Non-monthly Amount
Balance required in your Checking account		
Petty Cash		
Accounts Receivable		
Employee Advances		
Inventory		
Prepaid Expenses		
Deposits		
Land and Buildings		
Leasehold Improvements		
Equipment		
Computer Equipment		
Office Equipment		
Autos and Trucks		
Other Assets		
Intangibles (Patents, Trademarks)		
Cost of Sales – Wages		
Cost of Sales – Purchases		
Cost of Sales – Supplies		
Cost of Sales – Subcontractors		
Cost of Sales - Equipment Rental		
Cost of Sales – Other		
Salaries and Wages – Employees		
Salaries – Officers		
Bonuses		
Commissions		
Advertising and Marketing		
Recruiting		
Auto and Truck Expense		
Bank Service Charges		
Credit Card Processing Fees		
Credit Card Finance Charges		
General Insurance		
Life Insurance		
Liability Insurance		
Workmen's Compensation Insurance		
Interest Expense		
Legal Fees		
Accounting		
Office Supplies		
Postage and Delivery		
Freight		
Printing and Reproduction		

Fig. 8-4

Item	Monthly Amount	Non-monthly Amount
Dues and Subscriptions		
Seminars and Education		
Books and Publications		
Memberships		
Rent		
Equipment Rental		
Building Repairs and Maintenance		
Computer Repairs and Maintenance		
Equipment Repairs and Maintenance		
Janitorial Expenses		
Cleaning		
Sanitation		
Telephone		
Cellular Phone and Beeper		
Utilities – Gas		
Utilities – Electric		
Utilities - Water and Sewer		
Utilities – Other		
Internet Charges		
Miscellaneous		
Supplies		
Meals and Entertainment		
Travel		
Meeting Expenses		
Payroll Taxes		
Corporate Taxes		
Other State and Local Taxes		
Real Estate Taxes		
Licenses and Permits		
Employee Benefits - Medical Insurance		
Employee Benefits - Disability Insurance		
Employee Benefits - Life Insurance		
Employee Benefits – Retirement Plan costs		
Professional Fees		
Consultant Fees		
Contracted Services		
Payroll Service Company Fees		
Security Services/Systems		
Lease Payments		
Storage Charges		
Debt Collection		
Bad Debt Expense		
Laundry and Uniform Expense		

Pro forma financial statements

You can take the above budget projections one step further and create pro forma (Latin meaning "as a matter of form" or "as if") financial statements that project what a business's financial position or results will look like at a future time. Pro forma financial statements contain anticipated hypothetical financial results based on various assumptions.

ꝱꝱ

EXTRA HELP

The specific procedures for the creation of pro forma (projected) financial statements are outside the scope of this book. A good college-level accounting textbook or business financial analysis book will cover the steps for creating pro forma financial statements. However, depending on how developed or undeveloped your accounting skill set is, you may want a Certified Public Accountant (CPA) to create your pro forma financial statements.

ꝱꝱ

There are two basic pro forma financial statements you will need: an income statement and a balance sheet. Normally for a new business, pro forma income statements are produced each month for three years and then quarterly for the following two years, with an annual summary for each of these five years. The second pro forma financial statement is your balance sheet (also known as statement of financial position or statement of assets, liabilities and stockholder's equity), which should be created with the same timing (monthly, quarterly) you use to produce your pro forma income statements.

ꝱꝱ

BALANCE SHEETS

I must forewarn you that the main issue about creating pro forma balance sheets is that it involves a significantly greater amount of work than the creation of a pro forma income statement. This is because the projection of your balances in cash, accounts receivable, inventory, accounts payable, payroll taxes, and other liabilities is very difficult. Therefore, some business owners will produce a complete set of pro forma income statements, but instead of trying to create an actual set of pro forma balance sheets, they will create a pro forma cash-flow projection to forecast their financing needs by using an electronic spreadsheet package.

ȤȤ

Complete exercise 8-4 in workbook

Break-even analysis

A break-even analysis is a calculation of the point at which your revenue equals your expenses. It also shows how much profit or loss your business has at various levels of revenue. From a mathematical standpoint, it is a formula in which various parameters are substituted to compute a range or matrix of results, which are then often displayed in a graphical form. It is most often calculated by using an electronic spreadsheet software program like Microsoft Excel© or a financial analysis software program.

Your break-even point is calculated by separating budgeted or projected costs into three categories and then comparing the total of these costs to your revenue across the continuum of your revenue. You can also do this with your actual costs. Listed below are components of a break-even analysis:

Revenue—Total projected sales volume either on a monthly or annual basis.

Fixed costs—Costs that do not change over the normal range of your business's operations (e.g., office rent, liability insurance payments, utilities).

Semi-variable costs—Costs that increase in steps or plateaus. These are fixed for a certain range of operations and then they jump up a step. For instance, traditionally it is considered that a person can supervise up to eight people effectively; therefore, with one through eight employees you would have one supervisor but at nine employees, you would require two supervisors.

Variable costs—Costs that vary proportionately with your revenue (e.g., cost of sales materials, cost of sales labor costs, supplies, expenses). Most often these expenses are cost-of-sales expenses, but they can also consist of overhead expenses.

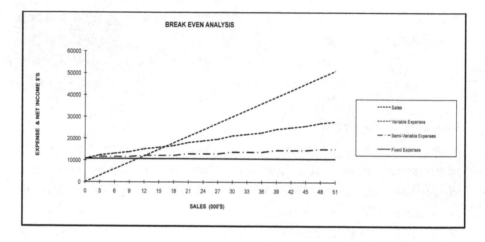

Fig. 8-5

The easiest way to identify and separate your fixed costs from your semi-variable and variable costs is to print out a copy of your business's chart of accounts and mark an F next to each account that is a fixed cost, an S next to each account that is a semi-variable cost, and a V next to each account that is a variable cost. The sum of fixed, semi-variable, and variable costs is then compared to revenue at various levels of sales to determine the break-even point. You should begin the comparison of your projected revenue to the total of your fixed, semi-variable, and variable costs at the point where your revenue, semi-variable, and variable costs are zero and then increment them proportionately from there. When the above data is graphically presented, you can see how much profit you would realize at certain levels of revenue or conversely how much loss you would incur.

ʐʐ

IMPORTANCE OF BREAK-EVEN ANALYSIS

I feel it is absolutely necessary for a business to perform a break-even analysis to know its break-even point and to know how much profit or loss it will realize or incur at various levels of revenue.

It should be noted that the lower your break-even point, the easier it is to obtain investors in your business because the revenue hurdle to make a profit is more achievable.

ʐʐ

Complete exercise 8-5 in workbook

TYPES OF FINANCING

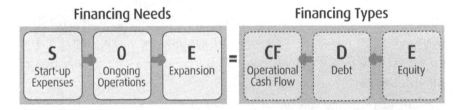

Fig. 8-6

A business can be financed in one of three ways: from the ongoing profits of the business, by borrowing money or from capital injected in the business. Obviously when a business first begins operations, there are no profits; therefore, a business requires initial funding from outside source(s). Once the business is fully operational, depending on the profitability of the business and its rate of growth, the future funding requirements may or may not be able to be met from the continuing operations of the business.

Operational Cash Flow

There are three factors that determine your ability to finance the growth of your business from its ongoing operations. These are your profitability, rate of asset growth and how much money is being withdrawn from the business by the owners.

If your business is extremely profitable then internally funding your growth is a viable option. Furthermore, if your business is profitable and your accounts receivable, inventory, and furniture, equipment and vehicles are not growing faster than your profitability is increasing, then depending on what your funding needs are, you may be able to generate the necessary cash flow from with inside the business. However, if your assets are growing at the same or a faster rate than your profitability is rising, it will not be possible to fund your business internally.

The third factor that must be considered is how much money are the business owners taking out of the business? If your business is very profitable, your asset growth is under control but the vast majority of available cash is being withdrawn from the business, the liquidity to fund your growth is not obtainable. In smaller businesses that is why it is so important to limit the amount of money which is being withdrawn by the business owners if that business has expansion desires. If this latter scenario is present, then unless the business sells some of its assets to raise funds, it will require outside financing.

Outside financing falls into one of two categories:

- Debt financing
- Equity financing

Debt Financing

This type of financing involves funds borrowed by the business that must be repaid. The term (length of time until the amount has to be fully repaid), the interest rate (if any), and all other provisions involving the loan should be explicitly spelled out in the loan agreement to prevent misunderstandings.

Generally, the interest amount being paid is a deductible expense for the business. As far as the repayment of the principal amount that has been lent to the business, it can be paid back to the lender either during the term of the loan or when the loan matures (known as a balloon payment). There are loans, notes payable, and bonds that start out as a debt of the business but are convertible to equity in a business.

Equity Financing

This type of financing involves funds that are more or less put into your business for the life of the business. Various terms can be used to describe this category of financing: equity, capital, stock, capital stock, common stock, preferred stock, additional paid in capital, etc. A business can only receive equity funding from an owner of the business—a non-owner cannot have an equity interest in a business. Therefore, if you want to obtain financing from a source and treat the funding as equity financing, you will need to issue an ownership stake in your business to that source.

ƶƶƶƶƶƶƶƶƶƶƶƶƶƶƶƶƶƶƶƶƶƶƶƶƶƶƶƶƶƶƶƶƶƶƶƶƶƶ

THE CROWN JEWEL

The ownership of your business is the crown jewel of your business. You should not provide ownership to your business to anyone beside yourself unless it is the last resort for funding your business.

ƶƶƶƶƶƶƶƶƶƶƶƶƶƶƶƶƶƶƶƶƶƶƶƶƶƶƶƶƶƶƶƶƶƶƶƶƶƶ

Consider your alternatives thoroughly before providing equity ownership in your business for your financing needs because by utilizing equity financing, you will almost assuredly have less control over your business going forward, and you will obtain less of the current and future financial benefits from your business.

Lastly, separate the ownership of your building or other assets (i.e., a fleet of trucks) from the funding of your operational business. This is because the financing of an asset is relatively straightforward and is not a strategic action; however, anything involving the funding of your business operation is strategic.

Complete exercise 8-6 in workbook

SOURCES OF FINANCING

Where can you obtain funding for your business? There are a large number of options but they basically fall into two categories: Owner financing (you fund the business yourself) and outside financing (others fund your business). Here is a checklist for each:

Owner Financing

- **Personal funds that you as an owner put into your business—** This may come from your checking account, savings account, or investments.

- **Refinancing your house**—Refinancing your residence for an amount greater than its current mortgage and placing the additional amount into your business.

- **Home equity loans**—Taking out a home equity loan or a home equity line of credit on real estate that you own.

- **Second mortgage**—Borrowing on your personal residence by taking out a second mortgage.

- **Loans on other assets**—Loans using any asset that you own personally (e.g., second home, automobile, boat, investments) as collateral. You borrow a certain percentage of the value of the automobile; if you default on the loan, the lender takes the auto.

- **Sale of personal assets**—Selling any personal asset and investing the proceeds in your business.

- **Personal loan from a bank**—There are many forms of borrowing funds personally from a bank or savings and loan association, so consult your local banker.

- **Loans from a family member or friend**—Funds loaned to you personally that you invest in your business.

- **Credit Cards**—Using personal credit cards to make purchases for the business or taking a cash advance and investing the funds in your business.

- **Investment amount from another existing owner**—Funds put into your business from any existing owner who is not yourself.

- **Selling equity (stock) in your business**—Funds put into your business from an investor who becomes a new owner of your business.
- **Accessing your retirement savings**—Investing in your business either: 1) directly by using a self-directed IRA (consult your tax advisor for the details of how to accomplish this) or 2) by taking a withdrawal or a loan from your qualified retirement account.
- **Borrowing on life insurance**—Taking a loan out against the cash surrender value on a life insurance policy, then placing the funds in your business
- **Selling assets** of the business that are not required for its operation.

Outside Financing

- **Customer Deposits**—An advance, deposit, retainer, or down payment from a customer who can be temporarily used for financing purposes.
- **Accounts Payable**—Your accounts payable balance is actually financing that is in essence provided by your vendors or suppliers.
- **Credit cards**—Using business credit cards to make purchases for the business or taking a cash advance and investing the funds into your business is a short-term funding tool.
- **Bank loans on the assets of the business**—Borrowing funds by using business assets pledged as collateral.
- **Bank loans to the business**—A loan or a line of credit to the business for which there is no collateral pledged by the business.
- **Loans or investments from your family or friends directly to your business**—This is known as the "friends and family plan." The biggest issue with this option is making sure you fully document whether the funds are debt or equity financing. Because of the nature of these types of investments, there can be great misunderstanding as a result of an entire host of assumptions made by the parties involved in the transaction.
- **Loan from a commercial finance company**—A loan or a line of credit to the business from a non-bank source for which no collateral has been pledged by the business.

- **SBA**—Guaranteed loans from a Small Business Administration (SBA) lender. These loans are issued by a bank or a qualified SBA lender, and the repayment is guaranteed by the SBA. At this time there are three main loan programs, namely: **7(a) Loan Guaranty, Certified Development Company (CDC) 504 Loan, and the Microloan 7(m) Loan.**

- **Angel investors**—Individuals or groups who lend money to or invest in businesses in various stages of their development (generally the amounts invested are less than the amounts invested by venture capital funds).

- **Venture capitalists or venture capital funds**—Individuals or entities who invest in businesses in various stages of their development (generally the amounts invested are greater than the amounts invested by angel investors).

- **Asset-based financing**—Financing based on the ongoing balance or collection of certain assets (e.g., accounts receivable, inventory) of the business (sometimes referred to as factoring).

- **Grants from various governmental or non-governmental entities**—Funds obtained as result of applying for a grant from a governmental or non-governmental organization.

- **Insurance policies**—A loan against the cash surrender value on a life insurance policy owned by the business.

- **Loan Brokers**—Third parties who arrange for loans from various sources.

- **Bartering services with someone**—While this is not really a financing source, by entering into a bartering relationship, you may conserve some cash, which in turn reduces the amount of financing you will require. Bear in mind that, conversely, you also will not receive cash from the product that you would have sold to your customer if you were not engaged in a bartering relationship.

- **Funding from a supplier**—Sometimes if a supplier or vendor has a vested interest in your business being successful, growing as one of their customers, or is generous, they may invest in or loan funds to your business.

ʑʑ

PERSONAL INVESTMENT IS KEY

If you do not have a significant amount personally invested in your business and you try to raise either debt or equity from an outside party, you may be faced with some very tough questions and a lot of rejections. Put yourself in their shoes: Imagine that your neighbor pitches a business to you and wants you to invest in it. You have some reservations, and then you find out that the neighbor has put little or none of his own money into the business. What would you do?

ʑʑ

Complete exercise 8-7 in workbook

EVALUATION OF FINANCING CRITERIA

Once you have determined the amount of financing you require and whether you will employ debt or equity funding (or a combination of both), the next step is to convince the person(s) or entity(ies) to actually provide the funding to your business. Therefore, it is prudent to be fully conversant with the factors they will use to evaluate your business with regard to financing your business. Of course, there are an almost unlimited number of factors that can be examined by a lender or investor to evaluate the risk versus the return of financing your business. However, there are seven main categories normally used to evaluate your business's financial situation:

1. The growth potential of your business
2. The level of risk involved in your business
3. The profit capabilities of your business
4. Whether they are considering making a debt or equity investment in your business

5. The rate of interest you will pay on a debt investment or the amount of ownership you will provide in return for equity financing

6. The length of time until you will repay the debt or provide a sufficient return on the equity

7. Your business's credit situation and history

Complete exercise 8-8 in workbook

OBTAINING FUNDING

Depending on the type of investment, amount of the investment, the complexity of your business situation, and the sophistication of the investor, you will need to create an information package for each potential investor. While this is not an exhaustive list of what would be included in a detailed investment information package, listed below are typical items included in an information packet for a debt investment from a bank:

- Business Loan Application Form
- A complete business plan
- Cash-flow projections
- Monthly financial projections for the next 12 months
- Quarterly or annual financial projections for years two and three
- A description of your accounting and recordkeeping systems
- A personal financial statement
- Personal tax returns (for the past two or three years)
- An accounts payable aging
- An accounts receivable aging
- An inventory status report (if applicable)
- Appraisals (if applicable)

ꙅꙅꙅꙅꙅꙅꙅꙅꙅꙅꙅꙅꙅꙅꙅꙅꙅꙅꙅꙅꙅꙅꙅꙅꙅꙅꙅꙅꙅꙅꙅꙅꙅꙅꙅꙅ

CONVERTING THE STRUCTURE OF PROFITABILITY™ INTO A TRADITIONAL BUSINESS PLAN

As we discussed back in Chapter 2, a traditional business plan is not easily implemented. Many times it ends up sitting on a shelf collecting dust because it is not actionable. However, the Structure of Profitability™ process that is the core of this book is fully actionable. Nevertheless, there are occasions where a traditional business plan is required. Most often this occurs because of needing outside financing; in this case, a traditional business plan becomes a necessity.

However, it is very easy to take the information that comprises the seven steps covered in this book, expand it, and place it in a traditional business-plan format. The easiest way to do this is to refer to the list at the end of Chapter 2 that describes what is typically included in a traditional business plan, or you can translate the seven steps of the Structure of Profitability™ into a traditional business plan.

ꙅꙅꙅꙅꙅꙅꙅꙅꙅꙅꙅꙅꙅꙅꙅꙅꙅꙅꙅꙅꙅꙅꙅꙅꙅꙅꙅꙅꙅꙅꙅꙅꙅꙅꙅ

Before you get to the stage of providing a detailed information package, a key step you may want to take is to create a one-page summary to provide a quick introduction to your business. Here is a list of the items that this one-page snapshot (your "One Sheet" or "Executive Summary") should look like:

- Your company name
- Your Vision Statement
- Description of your product
- Overview of your market
- Your Strategic Advantage
- Your Unique Selling Proposition (USP)
- Overview of your revenue model

- Your management team and personal qualifications
- The amount of the investment needed
- Projected use of the investment proceeds
- Summary-level financial projections

CONSULT AN ATTORNEY

Before you distribute any information in an effort to obtain financing for your business, consult an attorney to ensure you are complying with all applicable laws about supplying information to a potential investor.

Additionally, you should be able to present a summary of the following items in sixty seconds in an informal presentation of your business (not in front of an audience, but perhaps in a one-on-one conversation):

- Overview of your product
- Overview of your market
- Your Unique Selling Proposition (USP)
- Overview of your revenue model
- The amount of the investment needed

Whether it is a formal or informal presentation, the objective should be a specific action to be taken by your audience. That action may be: a financial commitment by them, a commitment to review some information you have provided them (and a follow-up discussion you will have with them), a referral to someone else who may be interested in investing in your business, or some other action you would like them to take.

In selecting an individual or organization from whom you wish to obtain financing, you should get answers to these types of questions before you enter into any serious discussions:

- Has the individual or entity had experience in providing funding to businesses? You do not want to be dealing with someone who may get cold feet and back out during the financing process; this can happen very easily with a novice investor.
- Does the individual or entity regularly provide funding to your size of business?
- If the source is an organization or a business, is this the size operation with which you want to do business? Are they too big and you might get lost in the shuffle? Are they too small and your needs will overwhelm their funding abilities?
- Does the individual or entity specialize in or shy away from providing funding to businesses in your industry?
- How extensive will the financing process be and the paperwork involved in dealing with this financing source?

Complete exercise 8-9 in workbook

UPDATING YOUR CRITICAL SUCCESS FACTORS

Back in Chapter 4 you identified the Critical Success Factors for your business. Now that you have completed analyzing the financing of your business area, you will want to review and if necessary, modify and/or add to the Critical Success Factors you have already identified.

ꝜꝜꝜꝜꝜꝜꝜꝜꝜꝜꝜꝜꝜꝜꝜꝜꝜꝜꝜꝜꝜꝜꝜꝜꝜꝜꝜꝜꝜꝜꝜꝜꝜꝜꝜꝜꝜꝜ

THE SOLUTION

I began to help Karen, who was concerned about her lack of understanding of the financial area of business. I explained that she only had three general needs for the financing of her business—the initial start-up expenses, the ongoing operations, and the expansion of her business. This caused her stress level to go down tremendously.

The first thing she did was to speak to her husband, who had started several businesses himself, and together they identified the initial start-up expenses and a general budget for her business. Next Karen approached a long-time friend in the home health industry about working with her on a consulting basis to develop initial monthly and annual budgets. This person also took budget information and used it to produce pro forma financial statements. Additionally, they created a break-even analysis that showed Karen specifically what revenue level the business would need to reach to begin to make a profit.

When she completed the above three steps, Karen was able to determine the amount of financing she needed for the business. As we discussed her financing options, she decided that since she had been successful in her career and her husband had been successful in his businesses, they could fund the business startup themselves. They would put some of the money in Karen's business as equity and some in as debt.

In doing one-, three-, and five-year projections for the business, Karen and her friend determined that she would most likely need outside financing by the time she was operating for five years. These projections proved to be correct. At the end of the first year in business, Karen had twenty-five employees, and by the second year, it had grown to fifty-five employees. During the first three years of operations, Karen and her accounting staff tracked her ongoing performance by comparing her financial results to her budget projections, pro forma financial statements and break-even analysis. At the end of three years, Karen had ninety-five employees and she was beginning to need additional funding to grow the business to a five-year target of two hundred employees and twenty million dollars in revenue.

As she looked forward to the future growth of her business, Karen started to consider how an outside financing source would evaluate her business with regard to its financial operations. From a growth standpoint, she had a very good track record; her business was generating above-average profit margins for the home health industry. Thereafter, she and her financial guru friend put together projections showing the future revenue and profit growth of the business and the risks that were involved with growing the business to the next level.

Karen considered both taking on debt for the business and also obtaining an equity investment from a group of investors. As a result of conversations we had, she decided to pursue equity financing. She put together a financing package for the potential equity investors that showed the amount of ownership she would provide in return for the equity financing. They liked the projections and the commensurate return on their investment, so they invested the amount of capital Karen required. Karen was overjoyed when her business went on to achieve her five-year goal of two hundred employees and twenty million dollars in revenue.

ZZZZZZZZZZZZZZZZZZZZZZZZZZZZZZZZZZZZZZZZZZZZZ

CHAPTER 9

STEP #7:
EXECUTION—
INNOVATING AND
SYSTEMATIZING

ƶƶ

THE CHALLENGE

Sun was a serious but friendly twenty-nine-year-old computer software engineer who had graduated from a prestigious university. Even though he had come to the United States from China to go college when he was eighteen, he spoke very good English. On graduating, he chose to stay in the United States to pursue his dream of being a business owner. Sun was one of six owners of a large computer software business that had operations in three states. Most of the six owners had gone to graduate school together for computer science degrees, so they were both friends and co-owners of the business. Sun was the major shareholder of the business, which specialized in software for the medical industry. They were now consumed with a project to produce a new generation of electronic health record software.

While the project was moving along well, their company was facing two challenges. The first was to coordinate the planning efforts of the six owners who were spread across three states. The second issue was how to properly plan for the future of their business and the software they provided, and then how to properly execute the plan. As software engineers, all six owners tended to be very task-oriented; they viewed meetings and formal planning activities as something to be avoided. Additionally, they enjoyed working on the details of a project instead of overseeing and directing others in completing the project or task.

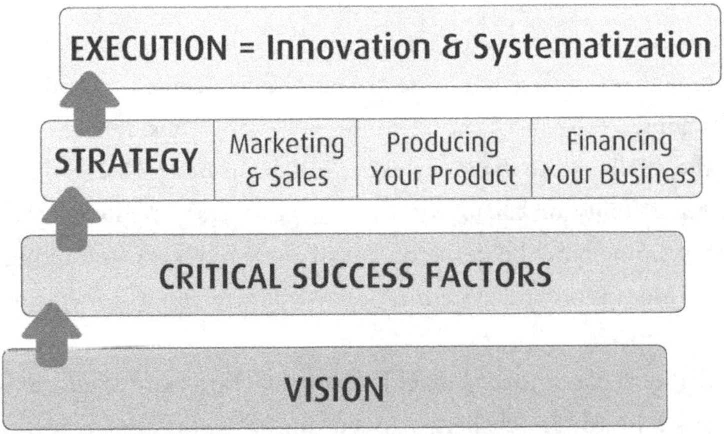

ʔʔ

Fig. 9-1

We are now at the seventh step in the Structure of Profitability process—the execution of the strategy for your business. This execution breaks down into two separate phases: 1) innovating your business, and 2) systematizing the operations of your business. Execution and its two components, innovation and systematization, are key to creating a business that is more than yourself.

If you are interested in any of the immediately following items, then this chapter is for you—the keys are all detailed here. We will look at how to achieve these and more in the forthcoming pages.

- Growing your business to one million, ten million, one-hundred million, or even a billion dollars
- Expanding your business overseas

- Franchising your business
- Taking your business to the next level
- Developing a game-changing, breakthrough product
- Using your business to change the world and make it a better place
- Working fewer hours in your business, but making more profit
- Passing your business on to your children
- Selling your business for a large profit and doing something different with the rest of your life

Doing big, great, innovative, or expansive things with your business does not start with execution but instead starts with detailed planning. Is your business going to be the same as millions of other businesses? Or will you accept the challenge to have an exceptional business? Does your business have the possibility or capability for true greatness? In this chapter we are going to examine how the development of these two keys to building a great business—innovation and systemization—will give you a strategic advantage in the marketplace.

With regard to greatness, I would like to give you a word of encouragement. We have all heard the challenge to become a world-class company or to become the best in the world. While these are lofty goals, as you implement the information in this chapter, focus first on becoming the best in your city, then the best in your county, next the best in your state, thereafter the best in your geographic area, after that the best in your country, and finally the best in the world. Just remember that this entire process begins by having realistic goals for your business toward which you can see some accomplishment in the near term.

BUSINESS PLANNING ACTIVITIES

Thus far we have discussed many items and issues about creating a thriving business. As you know from your personal experience and from the insights you have gained from reading this book, creating a thriving business does not just happen; it is accomplished as the result of planning, execution, and evaluation. Planning and evaluation require focused time to be done effectively; you need to set aside time for these things. There are three levels of "thinking about your business" time:

Level 1: Quick-thinking time

This is the time where you have some information about your business with you, or you are listening to an educational CD while you are driving. You are considering or thinking about your business for fifteen minutes, an hour maybe. There is no formal agenda and there may be no outcome, you are simply mulling over some aspect of your business. If you are reviewing information such as a marketing plan, list of issues, or a financial statement, what you really want is to contemplate the issue and your various courses of action. What is really happening in this time is that you are slowly incubating various options and trying to plant the seeds of solutions in your mind. If you are listening to an educational CD, tape, or other audio recording, what you want is to actively consider and possibly apply what you are hearing specifically to your business instead of passively listening to the recording. Keep in mind that "wasted" time in your vehicle or on an airplane or at the doctor's waiting room is time you can turn into productive planning time.

Complete exercise 9-1 in workbook

Level 2: Designated pondering time

This is a longer period of time where you go to a place where you can think without interruptions to address a particular issue or problem in your business. You have some specific information to review and think about. This pondering time should include a dose of being curious about your business. A business owner should be like a child—curious about everything. A one-year-old will examine anything and everything by handling it, pushing it, squeezing it, looking at it from various angles, dropping it, tasting it. Pondering involves saying to yourself, "What will happen if I do _____?" or "What if we tried _____?"

Generally the outcome from this type of stepping back and looking at your business from a different angle is a decision or a course of action you have now chosen because of the time involved in pondering.

Complete exercise 9-2 in workbook

Level 3: Dedicated planning time

This is formal, scheduled planning time for which you have ideally created some form of an agenda. Go to your favorite place to think, where you feel relaxed and peaceful. This designated planning time could be several hours to several days long, depending on the size and complexity of your business and the issues with which you are dealing. Why do I feel business owners need uninterrupted time for planning for their businesses? Think of the old analogy of not seeing the forest because you are so close to the trees. Without taking specific time to step back and avail yourself of a much broader perspective regarding your business, including the overall environment in which your business operates, you are liable to miss things that anyone looking at your business from a "forest" perspective would see. This "stepping back to consider" time includes utilizing dedicated business planning retreats.

Complete exercise 9-3 in workbook

DEVELOPING A GAME-CHANGING VISION

To avoid having an also-ran type of business that is merely okay or a business that is only able to pays the bills, you must have a game-changing Vision for your business, one that will be able to move your business from good to great. It is the kind of Vision that pushes your entire industry or business segment to operate differently because what you have developed is so far advanced compared to how your competitors function or the products they offer. Therefore, your competition either must change or risk falling by the wayside in the development and evolution of your industry.

What are the advantages of having a game-changing Vision? This kind of Vision for a business propels it forward toward operating in an optimal way.

A game-changing Vision takes what we discussed back in Chapter 3 regarding having a compelling Vision one step further and results in:

- Developing the North Star for your business that will guide you well into the future
- Creating a business that raises the bar and provides a "win" for each of your business's five stakeholders
- Having the "fire in your belly" that motivates you each day to continue to work on making your business operate the way you want it to perform
- Delivering your product/service so that each of your Customers will truly walk away with an experience from you business "worth repeating"

To develop a game-changing Vision, you must reset your initial Vision for your business. I refer to this resetting as revisioning because you are essentially revising your original Vision. Consequently, you use the same process to revise your Vision as you used to develop your original Vision. If you recall back in Chapter 3, we discussed the concept that everything related to your business (this is also true for other things in your life) should be created three times: First in your mind, then on "paper," then in the real world. This progression applies directly to the Revisioning process; the recreation of your business should first take place in your mind. You can then transfer your renewed Vision to paper or electronic media so you can begin to transform your current business from where is it currently to what you want it to be!

In Chapter 3 we also discussed that there are three steps in the creation of a compelling Vision for your business. We called these the three C's of Visioning:

- Conceptualizing what your business is all about
- Crafting a compelling vision
- Casting your vision

To continually renew your Vision for your business, you need to turn these steps into a structured process and apply the three C's of Visioning to your business in a systematic way.

The process of developing a game-changing vision for your business

There are five steps to developing a game-changing Vision for your business. These are:

1. Determine what would be the "ideal solution" for your Customer.
2. Narrow the ideal solution to a certain price level or target market.
3. Decide what you are willing to change to provide the ideal or improved solution to your Customer.
4. Develop the systems to deliver the improved solution.
5. Identify other changes you would need to make to provide the solution upon which you have decided.

Determining the ideal solution for your Customer

I have found that an easy way to jumpstart the reconceptualizing process is to reflect on or ponder about how the world ought to be or how the world ought to work in the context of the environment in which your business operates. Specifically, you want to focus on your Customers and envision the best way they could have their need met by your product?

At this point in your reconceptualizing process, absolutely do not limit or consider the meeting of your Customer's needs in the context of how your existing business operates—in fact, it may be helpful to pretend that your business does not even exist! In essence, imagine in a perfect world the best possible way that your Customer's goals could be met. This will require you to expand your thinking and develop your thoughts regarding how an ideal world would operate pertaining to your market and your Customer's needs being fulfilled. In imagining how the world ought to operate, it may be useful to reflect on the "true values" of life, the "truths of life," the entire concept of excellence, and how excellence would be manifested in your market.

Here are ten innovations from 1995 to 2010 where someone asked, "What is the best way that our customers' needs can be met?

1. iPod
2. YouTube
3. Smart phones
4. Groupon
6. Facebook
7. All-electric cars
8. Civilian hypersonic aircraft for space tourism
9. Apps for smart phones
10. Civilian use of GPS

Keep in mind that improving your solution and moving your solution (your product) toward the ideal solution for your Customer may also involve small or incremental steps. Some examples are:

- A plastic sheet inside the top of an ice cream carton to keep it from icing
- Restaurant pagers that let you know your table is ready
- Banking hours on evenings and weekends
- Upside-down condiment bottles with flat caps for easy dispensing
- Prescription bottle-cap medication reminder systems that use the internet
- Civil courts of law with evening hours so people do not have to miss work
- Pre-ordering food online for pickup at restaurants
- Customer loyalty shopping cards
- 24-hour stores
- Foam tip applicators on bottles of Wite-Out®

To properly complete the reconceptualizing process, you must first examine and determine the ideal solution from an *unconstrained* point of view; you want to think outside the box and not limit your possibility thinking. By thinking about all the various options that could meet your Customers' needs, you will be able to generate the greatest number of options, possibilities, and alternatives for enabling your Customers to achieve their goals. While some of these ideas may be unrealistic from a technical standpoint or pricing perspective, the ideas will spawn other ideas, thoughts, and concepts that may be more practical. One way of looking at this step is that it is a uniquely targeted method of brainstorming related to what you can do with your business. The outcome from this uniquely defined and constructed method of brainstorming then is eligible to become your renewed Vision for your business.

Keep in mind that the above process may not yield just one ideal solution; it may present multiple ideal solutions. In fact, this exercise of looking at how the world ought to work may provide you with an array of options, which may include variants of ideal solutions. At this point in the exercise, do not let your possibility thinking be constrained by costs to deliver or price points in your market; the goal is to develop as many excellent ideal solutions as possible.

Related to the above, keep in mind that to fully understand what your Customers' needs are and how they sense their needs, you must get inside their hearts and minds. To fully comprehend your Customers' needs, you must understand and address their perceived short-term, intermediate, and long-term goals, and the related emotional state that they perceive they want to be in as a result of achieving their goals. This entire concept of getting inside your Customer's heart and mind is part of the process of developing your Unique Selling Proposition (USP) that we discussed in Chapters 3, 5, and 6.

Complete exercise 9-4 in workbook

Narrowing the ideal solution to a certain price level or target market

Keeping in mind what was just discussed—how ought the world to work, what are your Customers' perceived goals, and getting inside your Customers' minds to fully understand the emotional state they want to be in as a result of purchasing your product—you can do the one thing that great visionaries and leaders do, which is to zero in on the *true* need of their target buyer. This will enable you to capitalize on this need by providing the best possible solution at a particular price level!

Now in reality you are not necessarily trying to provide the absolute best solution or a completely perfect solution to your Customer's need, unless your Customer has an unlimited budget for your product. You are trying to provide the best solution at a specific price point.

Once the first step has been completed, the second step is to narrow your ideal solution down to become the best solution that can be provided at a certain price level or to a particular target market that has product pricing constraints. Keep in mind that just like you did in step one, in this second step you are ignoring your current business and are not taking into account how you currently operate.

Let us look at an example of this narrowing process. Assume that you are a "dollar" store and you are going through this process to find new products you wish to carry, creating an improved business model. You have developed an array of ideal solutions for meeting your Customers' needs. Some of the options you have unearthed would require you to change the core way you are doing business or perhaps refocus your business on a different target market. Unless, as result of this process, you want to change your Vision for your business and try to become a higher-priced store, what we are talking about in this step is to choose only options or solutions that are consistent with your current target market. The result of this selection process is that you narrow down the list and choose from the various ideal solutions and related variants you have envisioned.

Consequently, you would choose the most attractive option that enables you to offer solutions at a certain price level to a specific target market, which in this example would be the target market for people spending only a dollar. So, once you have completed your possibility thinking you should only consider solutions that fall within your price level or target market (i.e., you could not sell furniture at a dollar store) unless one or more of the ideal solution options you have generated is so attractive that you decide to change the overall Vision for your business. By the way, if you have read the book *Good to Great* by Jim Collins, Kimberly-Clark's action of selling all their paper mills and moving into the consumer products arena is an example of a business changing its Vision because another business model was more attractive.

Let's look at another example. Say that you are a mid-priced cruise ship line, and you are completing this reconceptualizing process. As part of this second step, you will be evaluating your business with the target of providing the absolute best solution to your Customer at a mid-market price level, not a luxury cruise line price level. During step one, you should consider all the ways you could better serve your Customers, no matter what the cost, even if a certain idea or option does not fit in your pricing range as a mid-price cruise line. This is because during this second step you may be able to modify an idea enough to provide an improved solution to your current Customer within the pricing constraints.

The intended result of working through the above process is that you develop a concept for your business that would deliver the absolute best solution to your Customer at a certain price level. By deciding what future ideal solution you will provide to your target Customer, you are re-conceptualizing your business. Bear in mind as you are completing this endeavor, the absolute best solution you can provide to your Customer at a certain price level may change over time with advances in technology or changes in the environment, energy, social, or political arenas affecting your market. Consequently, one of your roles as the leader of your business is to keep an eye on these and other frontiers to evaluate how these changes may affect your ideal or perfect solution.

Complete exercise 9-5 in workbook

Deciding what you are willing to change in your business to provide an improved solution to your Customer

The third phase in this revisioning process is to come back to the real world, consider where your business is currently, and start to visualize how your business could provide this ideal solution. This third step requires you to look at the personality of your business and its available resources in the context of being able to produce and deliver this ideal or perfect solution. This step also requires you to assess how willing you are to possibly change your entire business philosophy, business model, and operations in order to be the source of an ideal solution to your Customer's need.

The above process of envisioning, consideration, analysis, and deliberation should lead you to make decisions about how far you are willing to go in the process of creating an ideal solution to your Customers' needs. This third step automatically yields a continuum of options that is available to you as a business owner. You could choose to make the commitment to totally transform your business to be the provider of the ideal solution for your Customer (which may also require you to transform your Delivery Channel). Alternatively, you could choose to do nothing at all. Or you could choose to do something in between. Included in this continuum of options are various incremental approaches to moving your current solution toward the ideal solution.

During the above steps you may have discovered that your current product can be applied to a new market or that a market that is different from your current market is very attractive. These two scenarios present you with the possibility of changing your business to focus on a new or different market for your product. There are countless examples of businesses totally re-inventing themselves (including many of the Fortune one-thousand companies) and emerging from this reconceptualizing process as a completely different business! Related to this discussion is the fact that many businesses define their business sector much too narrowly, which stifles and limits defining their original Vision, hampers the revisioning process, and restricts innovation. For instance, you are not in the automobile business but the transportation business, which involves electric cars, airplanes, trains, et al. Or, you are not in the oil and gas business but the energy business, which involves solar, wind, geothermal, et al.

If you choose to do nothing at all or something in between, it is important to note that you will then face two risks. First, if you don't provide the ideal solution or at least a better solution than is currently present in the marketplace, then your competitors might. Second, if the option you choose to pursue does not sufficiently improve your product, you run the risk that your improved solution may be perceived by your Customer as being an insignificant change. If this occurs then the work, effort, and cost you incurred to change your business to provide a better solution will not have your desired outcome, and it could result in a waste of your business's resources.

From a theoretical standpoint, the net financial effect from reconceptualizing your Vision is a result of: your business's perceived desire for change times the attractiveness of the new Vision minus the costs to change your business to achieve the renewed Vision. This means if there is a lack of desire for change within your business (and you do not or cannot convince your employees of your business's need for change), or the reconceptualizing of your Vision is not attractive enough to your target market (or the costs to change your business to achieve the renewed Vision are greater than the benefit), then the net financial result of changing your business could be negative. Therefore, you need to prudently and carefully go through this Vision reconceptualizing process.

If you are not totally pleased with the outcome from completing steps one, two, and three, it is possible to cycle through the entire process a number of times until you decide the best place to be on the continuum of creating the ultimate and ideal solution for your Customer before deciding on your renewed Vision for your business. It is important to remember that during this process you are focusing on creating the ideal solution for your target Customer at a certain price level or an alternative target market that will help you decide what actions to take regarding your product in the future.

As part of this reconceptualizing process, a parallel activity you may find very useful is to pretend you are your Customer and ask yourself, Would I buy this product or service? To obtain value from this parallel exercise you must be brutally frank with yourself because it will provide you with tremendous insights into your business by showing you the gap between how you think you are meeting your Customers' perceived needs and the solution your Customers feel you are providing them. If you would not buy your own product or service, then you need to start thinking about what do you need to change within your business to induce you to want to buy your own product or service! An objective way to obtain information from this additional activity is to hire secret shoppers or have a survey done of your current Customers.

Complete exercise 9-6 in workbook

Develop the systems to deliver the improved solution

The fourth step in this process is the development of the systems necessary to implement the changes required to deliver the improved solution to your Customer. Throughout this book we have discussed the concept of systematizing your business, particularly systematizing your Production area. Once you have decided on the product you wish to deliver in the future, the next step is to design, implement, and perfect the methodology for delivering this product. In reality, I am referring to the optimization of your product delivery system so it can provide the most desirable solution at a certain price level or to a specific market.

To supply this more desirable solution to your Customer, you must engineer into the system the quality and other attributes that your improved product must contain so that your business can produce the product. By concentrating on the optimization of the system that will be used to provide the new ideal product, you will as a consequence perfect both the product and the system that provides it.

If during the design, implementation, and evaluation stages for changing your systems, you observe that your product falls short of the quality and other attributes you have targeted to be delivered to your Customer, you will need to go back to the drawing board. Remember, the proper delivery of your new ideal product involves providing the target level of quality and other attributes one hundred percent of the time to take your business to a higher level.

Complete exercise 9-7 in workbook

Identifying other changes you need to make in your business to provide the solution upon which you have decided

At this point in the reconceptualizing process it is wise to take a step back and consider what other things in your business you may wish to change in conjunction with providing an improved solution (a renewed Vision) to your Customer. To do this, once you have decided on what improved or ideal solution you will be providing, you then need to re-examine your Critical Success Factors to determine if any of them require updating.

If your recalibrated Vision is basically going in the same direction as your previous Vision, then most likely you will not have to revise your Critical Success Factors. However, if you are making any substantial change to the direction of your business as reflected in its Vision, then most likely you will need to evaluate and possibly modify your Critical Success Factors. Furthermore, if you are making substantial changes to your Vision and your Critical Success Factors, you will want to fully review the details of your Strategy, which we laid out in Chapters 5 through 8.

Complete exercise 9-8 in workbook

RECRAFTING AND RECASTING YOUR VISION

The next step in developing a game-changing Vision for your business is to recraft and recast your Vision. This step utilizes pondering about your business in conjunction with the outcome from developing a renewed Vision for your business we just completed. Part of the pondering process is to mentally play with and ponder (ponder is a key word in this process) the mental images that were fundamental in helping you reconceptualize your business, what your ideal solution will look like when it is fully completed, and how your business will operate in the future.

Recrafting or recreating your Vision involves examining in detail the words and concepts in your current Vision and determining if they should be changed as a result of your renewed Vision. If the process of delivering your ideal solution and its benefits to your Customer will not be much different than they were previously, then your existing Vision statement may not need to be recrafted. However, if there will be substantial changes to your solution, then you want to capture the essence of the new and improved "win" you will be providing to your Customer by updating and changing the wording of your Vision statement.

Even if the outcome from the renewing of your Vision does not substantially change your overall Vision, you still may want to improve, enhance, and further develop your current Vision statement. The pondering process may have brought other thoughts, paradigms, and word pictures to mind regarding your solution and Vision for your business that you can now use to improve and reinforce the communication of your Vision. Keep in mind, as we discussed back in Chapter 3, your Vision is not magical—it will not automatically create a business that is the embodiment of your Vision. Instead, a properly crafted Vision guides and directs you and your personnel toward achieving that Vision for your business.

The goal is to use the outcome from these pondering or brainstorming times to come up with improved themes you can employ in your Vision. The pondering process may also present you with variations on the themes that were part of your original Vision.

As you go through this process, make sure you explore these thoughts, paradigms, and word pictures; test them in your mind to see if they reinforce or detract from your Vision statement. Ask yourself: "Do these other things harmonize with my Vision statement so I can use them to elaborate on my Vision statement, making it clearer and more attractive to my target audience?"

Last, practice using these words and images so you will be able to better communicate, i.e., recast your Vision.

Complete exercise 9-9 in workbook

INNOVATION

Innovation is the key to changing your business, enabling it to thrive and grow even more in the future. There is an increasing recognition that we have now moved from the technological revolution, through the information revolution, and on to the innovation revolution where societies and businesses will rise and fall based on their ability to quickly innovate themselves. Consequently, the more and faster that you can develop innovations and improvements in your business, the greater the number of Customers you will be able to service and the more you will be able to beat your competition.

But first we must define the term innovation. Webster's dictionary defines innovation as the creation or improvement of "products, technologies, or ideas." This includes the introduction of new products or methods as well as making changes to anything that is already established. Innovation is closely associated with increased productivity; it is a fundamental source of increasing wealth to an individual or in an overall economy. Furthermore, the persons who develop innovation are often referred to as pioneers in their field.

You can change and catapult your business forward by fostering an innovative business and work environment. This is done by encouraging the creation or improvement of your products, technologies, and processes. Innovation should take place throughout your business, not just in your Production or R&D areas. You can experience innovation in your Marketing area, in your Sales Processes, with the Delivery of your Product, using your Customer Service, in the Financing of Your Business as part of your Vision. Innovation should be present from the top of your business to the bottom and from the bottom of your organization to the top.

INNOVATE TO STAY COMPETITIVE

One of the key areas in which innovation should be present is the development of new products or improvement to your current products because your competition is always, always trying to get ahead of you.

Innovation does not simply happen in a business. Management must set innovation in stone as a foundational mindset throughout its business. Your personnel should be regularly trained and retrained on how to practice innovation and tap into their ingenuity and creativity. And you must foster and reward innovation, both financially and non-financially. Innovation should not be optional in your business; it should be required as basis of employment regardless of the role or task of the person.

Trying to cover the many aspects of developing innovation in business and the workplace is outside the scope of this book, but since I have considerable experience in this area, it will be the topic of a future book. In the meantime, there are two tools I will cover here related to innovation.

The first is one that we have already discussed—the concept of thinking about how the world ought to work and then developing the ideal solution for your Customer. The second tool is to look at every problem that occurs in your life as an opportunity for an innovation or an invention. Most people view the problems they incur during the day strictly as an irritation. However, you will operate very differently if you say to yourself, "Everything and anything in my day that does not go perfectly smoothly is a problem crying for a solution." Once you have this mindset, virtually every minute of every day becomes a laboratory for innovation. By using this approach you can unleash each of your personnel's creativity to solve various problems and thereby promote innovation within your business.

Bear in mind that innovation and technology can and do act like a catalyst for each other. Developments in technology enable and foster more innovation and innovation spawns technology. Once the mindset of innovation has been put in place, this cycle of innovation and technology can become a self-perpetuating process.

INNOVATION = WEALTH

History tells us that innovation leads to true wealth, and that the future businesses and societies that are the best innovators will economically lead the world.

Complete exercise 9-10 in workbook

FRUIT STANDS VERSUS FACTORIES

Earlier in this chapter we discussed the need for optimizing your systems in the context of implementing your renewed Vision for your business. Now let's expand that discussion and look at the details involved in optimizing your systems so you are able to create a thriving business. Why are systems so important and crucial?

Having worked with over twelve hundred businesses in the past fifteen years, I have found that there are basically two ways in which a business can operate—a fruit stand model and a factory model. In the fruit stand model, the fruit-stand owner shows up Monday, Tuesday and Wednesday and sets out the fruit, sells the fruit, and has revenue. However, on Thursday the owner does not show up; consequently there is no revenue because there was no one there to set out the fruit. Friday the owner returns, sets out the fruit, sells it and has revenue. Under the fruit-stand model, the business is more or less totally dependent on the owner. If they are not there to do certain tasks or to enforce others to do them, or to scold their personnel for doing these tasks the wrong way, the business does not operate properly.

Conversely, in the factory model the owner shows up Monday and builds the factory, but has no revenue. Tuesday they come in, hire the personnel, train them, and put the equipment in place, but still there is no revenue. On Wednesday they come in, start the factory, oversee operations, and have revenue. Thursday they come in, oversee operations, and have revenue. However, on Friday they do not show up, but they still have revenue. The next Monday they do not show up, but they still revenue. Under the "economic" factory model, the business takes the time to develop, implement, and optimize the systems that are necessary for the business to operate on its own. It takes more time and effort on the front end of a business to develop a factory-type business; however, the business ends up not being dependent on the business owner for its daily operations, which frees up the business owner to work *on* the business instead of being fully consumed working *in* the business.

Here are the attributes of a fruit-stand type of business:

- The business has not been fully systematized.
- The business is not scalable and it is difficult to grow the business to the next level.
- The business is overly dependent on the business owner.

Here are the attributes of a factory type of business:

- The business has been fully systematized.
- The business is scalable and it is not overly difficult to grow to the next level.
- The business is not overly dependent on the business owner.

Systems are the key to transforming your business from a fruit stand to a factory!

zzzzzzzzzzzzzzzzzzzzzzzzzzzzzzzzzzzzzzzzzzzzzzz
AN ECONOMIC FACTORY

When I say factory, I do not mean a sweat shop or a grungy, dirty factory, but instead a clean, well-lit, exciting, and enjoyable place to work—like a gleaming new car factory or an airplane factory. It is a fully systematized business that operates correctly, is a pleasure for employees to work there, a joy for the owners to operate, and a delight for the Customers— that is an economic factory.

zzzzzzzzzzzzzzzzzzzzzzzzzzzzzzzzzzzzzzzzzzzzzzz

Complete exercise 9-11 in workbook

SYSTEMS
Throughout these pages we have discussed the need for systems within your business and for taking a systematic view of your business. The Systems for your business are comprised of your overall and general plans and your specific and detailed processes.

Plans
Your plans state how you want things to operate within your business at the general level. Your plans are related to each of the areas of your business. From an overall standpoint, they state what your methodology will be for accomplishing tasks within your business. From a conceptual standpoint, your personal philosophical underpinnings determine how you would like your

business to operate (your plans), and therefore your plans are developed with your philosophies and principles in mind.

Processes

While your plans lay out the overall blueprint for the operation of each of the areas of your business, the exact details of your plans are specified in your processes. Therefore, the second part of your Systems is your processes. Processes are written documents that identify the necessary steps to follow to produce effective performance in each area. They need to specify a sequential set of actions to be taken to produce a consistently desired result.

Your processes include the exact details of how you will accomplish your plans in each of the areas of your business. Since they are in essence an extension of your plans, they need to be completely in synch with them. Your processes need to include the step-by-step directions about what must be done to obtain the desired outcome you have stated in your plans. Your processes are the executable portions of the Systems of your business. They need to specify how everything is done within your business and who does it.

A Process should be developed and documented for everything in your business. Your Processes could range from opening your business in the morning, closing it at night, how you do competitive market research, the details of your sales efforts, how you create or develop your Product, how you close your accounting records at the end of each month, how you organize and carry out your planning retreats. Thus you can see that your Systems and their detailed Processes are key for your business. There are three steps that must be completed with regard to your Processes: 1) identify your Processes, 2) optimize your Processes and 3) fully document your Processes.

We have discussed why Systems are so important to a business, but why are Processes so important? To achieve the goal of fully satisfying your Customer one hundred percent of the time, you must have systems in place that ensure a quality product is being delivered to your Customer. Without the correct systems in place, invariably you will end up with inconsistent results, which will lead to Customer dissatisfaction and cause you to not reach your Vision for your business. If you truly distill a business down to what value it is providing to its Customer, that value originates from the Processes of the business. By systematizing your business through the use of optimized and documented Processes, you will be able to ensure that as your business's volume grows, your Product quality does not decrease.

Complete exercise 9-12 in workbook

Development of your Processes

There are four fundamental keys to defining the Processes for your business.

1. Develop optimized Processes for *all* the activities, actions, and events that take place within your business.

2. Document each step of every Process in writing; nothing is left to chance for the executer of the Process to figure out on their own or alternatively to make their own decisions. Instead, detailed step-by-step directions are provided to the personnel who are executing the Process.

3. Personnel are fully trained on the Processes in which they are involved.

4. Personnel use the Processes on a consistent basis and the written Processes are available to the personnel executing the process for periodic review.

In trying to gain a full understanding of this concept of Processes, the analogy can be of used of comparing the fruit stand to the economic factory we discussed earlier. Most businesses start out by going through the absolutely normal phase of being a "fruit stand" during which the business owner is trying to figure out the business. During this time, the solidification of the processes for the business should be taking place. A pattern of trial-and-error effort is typical during this phase, which leads to discovering what works and what does not work. An indicator that your business is moving from the fruit stand to a factory mode is the solidification of the processes for your business.

After this initial phase of systematizing your business, you want to continue creating the best Processes to optimize your Systems. When you are first solidifying your Processes or if you have none, an excellent way to developing optimal Processes is to gather all the persons who are involved in a particular area and as a team determine the best system. Let's say you have five salespersons and up to now you have let each one fulfill their sales responsibilities as they saw fit. You have one superstar sales person, one very good sales person, two average sales persons, and one below-average sales person. By getting all five of your sales persons in the room together with you and having each person share in detail how they execute their sales activities, you can jointly determine the optimal sales Process and obtain buy-in from each of them as they provide input to and formulate the optimal sales Process.

A key part of documenting the final optimized Process is to record why the Process was solidified as it was, so any and all future users of the Process understand the background of solidifying the Process, the detailed analysis and logic that were used to develop the current Process. When all users are included in defining the Process, they are less likely to question the Process and more likely to adhere to it.

Periodically the team that defined the Process or a group of people that represent the users of the subject Process should have a meeting to discuss any suggested improvements to the Process or suggestions that relate to the Process. No changes should be used until the entire group has approved the change. Related to the above continuous improvement of your Processes is the recognition that there is an ongoing cycle between innovation and systematization. That is, you innovate and then systematize, then you innovate and then systematize.

Complete exercise 9-13 in workbook

YOUR DAILY ROLE IN YOUR BUSINESS

How do you apply these concepts to what you do as a business owner in your business on a daily basis? Many business owners ask me: "What should be my role in my business?"

No matter what the size of the business—small, medium, or large—there are two things that every business owner must do for their business on an ongoing basis. First is to live, eat, and breathe the Vision for their business. This task encompasses all we have covered with regard to guiding and directing the business. Second, they should oversee and manage the operations of their business by the use of Systems. Any and all business owners must do the above two things for their business to thrive!

These two tasks fall clearly within the realm of working *on* the business. But if your business is a smaller business (under fifteen million dollars or so in annual revenue) then most likely you will be working *in* the business. In my experience, once a business is over fifteen million dollars or so in annual revenues, seldom do we see a business owner work *in* the business because the responsibilities of working *on* the business take all their time. However, let me emphasize that if your business is a smaller size, you must make sure you do not get caught in the "tyranny-of-the-urgent syndrome" and get trapped only working *in* your business, therefore neglecting to work *on* your business.

Working *in* your Marketing and Sales area

If your business is the size where you will not only be working *on* the business but working *in* the business, in what should you be working? I feel that the most important "working in the business" role in which a business owner can be involved is to work within their Marketing and Sales area. Marketing and Sales is the lifeblood of every business; if you produce the best product but you cannot convince someone to buy your product, what use is your business? Marketing and Sales drives everything in your business—without sales you have no revenue, and without revenue you do not have a business.

You are your business's most effective salesperson because no one will have the passion for your product that you have; that passion will always become obvious in both the Marketing and the Sales processes of your business. This results in you being your business's most insightful marketer and best sales rainmaker. Additionally, because you are the business owner, you will know your products better than anyone else, and this will translate to more and better sales of your product. Another tremendous benefit of working in your Marketing and Sales area is that you can see firsthand what works and what does not work in your Marketing and Sales processes and therefore you can change, refine, and fully systematize your business's Marketing and Sales operations.

A side benefit of being involved in your Marketing and Sales operations is that it gives you the opportunity to get unique feedback from your Customers and prospects as to what they like about your product, what they do not like, improvements that can be made, and new products they may view with interest. This benefit ties back to your unique role of being the "scout" for your business, where you are looking down the road to guide your business where it should be going in the future. Therefore, I believe Marketing and Sales is the best area in which you can apply your leadership skill set if you are in fact working *in* your business.

There is one huge challenge for you if you regularly have Customer or prospect interaction while working in your Marketing and Sales area—Customers or prospects will view you personally as the Marketing and Sales operation of your business, may only want to deal with you personally, and will perceive your business as more of a fruit stand where *you* are the business instead of a factory where you are overseeing your operations.

The way to avoid this is to communicate with everyone with whom you interact that you are just a person in the Marketing and Sales area, anyone can do your job, you could step out of your Marketing and Sales role at any time and anyone else can take over what you are doing. Regularly taking other marketing and sales personnel out with you on marketing efforts and sales calls, operating your sales function like a team where you regularly hand the ball off to someone else, and having someone else take over as soon as the sale is made will demonstrate to the Customer that you are just a part of the Marketing and Sales team, and things can and do operate perfectly fine without you.

Working *in* your Production area

Some people are not comfortable in a Marketing and Sales role. If you have tried but you cannot get over that hurdle of doing Marketing and Sales, then the second best place to be working in the business is your Production area.

Keep in mind that while you may be focusing on your Production area and dealing with the operations of your business, you never really stop selling your business because you will always be casting your business's compelling Vision to someone.

The Production area is the second most important area of your business because your business could have sales going through the roof, but if you cannot provide the product that meets or exceeds your Customers' expectations, then your business will quickly fail. The entire area of Production is critical to your business; as the business owner, you know your product better than anyone else, putting you in a unique position to ensure that your product is of the quality you desire. Also, by utilizing your knowledge of your product and your Customers' goals, you should be able to further develop your Strategic Advantage and ensure you are creating an experience worth repeating for your Customer.

If you choose to make your Production area the section in which you work in the business, an additional benefit you should obtain from being directly involved in the Production area is that you should discover new ways to innovate your Production processes, systematize its operations, and perhaps develop new products—all of which will lead to making your business's solutions (products) more attractive to your Customer. Optionally, you could split your time between these two areas and spend your time working in both your Marketing and Sales area and your Production area.

Working in various sized businesses

If you are still in the start-up phase of your business and, therefore, most likely are still operating as a fruit stand, you should spend fifty percent of your time in your Marketing and Sales area and the majority of your other time in your Production area, ensuring that your product is being delivered properly. A significant portion of the time spent in your Marketing and Sales and Production areas should involve systematizing these areas.

As a start-up business, one of your chief priorities should be developing, optimizing, and documenting your systems. Innovation and systematization are the keys to moving your business from a fruit stand to a factory, thereby taking your business to the next level. Of course, you still need to spend sufficient time in your Finance and Administration, Human Assets, and Information Technology areas to ensure they are running properly, but they are the tail not the head of the dog, so be careful not to misplace your priorities.

The rule of thumb I use for start-up businesses is that for the first three years of the business, you are just figuring out the business out. This involves a trial-and-error process to determine what works and what does not work. This means that you must determine what makes your Customers happy versus what disappoints your Customers, and what causes problems for you and your business. You need to figure out what works, and then systematize it so you can move your business to an economic factory model. The goal is to identify and establish a business model that works properly. Properly and fully developing your Systems and then executing those Systems is absolutely fundamental to developing a great business model and moving you from working in your business to working on your business. Alternatively, if you fail to properly systematize your business and end up staying in the daily operations, your business will invariably stay as a fruit-stand type of business versus moving to a factory model.

If you have grown to the point where you have delegated (not abdicated) these areas to someone else, you should be overseeing the execution of your Marketing and Sales, Production, Finance and Administration, Human Assets, and Information Technology areas through the use of Systems as we discussed in this chapter. As far as time allocation is concerned, the important thing to keep in mind is that you need to spend the time to understand what works in your Marketing and Sales area and your Production area and then systematize them so you can move your business into operating as an economic factory. Of course, underlying this entire discussion is the foundational concept that no matter what size your business is, you need to be eating, sleeping, and breathing your Vision and guiding your business to that Vision.

Complete exercise 9-14 in workbook

UPDATING YOUR CRITICAL SUCCESS FACTORS

Back in Chapter 4 you identified the Critical Success Factors for your business. Now that you have completed analyzing your execution area, next review and, if necessary, modify and/or add to the Critical Success Factors you have already identified.

ʔʔʔ

THE SOLUTION

After we began to work together, the six business owners of the Electronic Health Record business saw that they were getting trapped in the "tyranny of the urgent." They concluded that whether they liked it or not, they needed to dedicate more time to planning activities—both individual and group planning. They decided each business owner would set aside two hours a week just to think about the business, ponder what was going on inside the business, and plot out where they wanted to take the business. Second, they decided they wanted formal and dedicated business planning meetings once a quarter in the form of a business planning retreat. After their first retreat, they realized it was almost a miracle their business had been as successful as it had been without this process.

During the planning retreats, as the owners began to tackle the issues involving the future of their business and their software, they began asking "how the world ought to work" with regard to what their Customers were trying to achieve and what was the best way this could be accomplished. This mode of thinking enabled them to start thinking in terms of what would be the ideal solution for their Customer.

As they recrafted their business in order to develop the systems necessary to deliver these improved software solutions, they also looked for ways to innovate their business to the next level. As they focused on developing the systems and then overseeing the operation of the systems, the execution of their overall strategy became very logical and straightforward. By concentrating on the innovation and execution of their systems, they were able to create software for the new generation of Electronic Health Records.

This all led them to focus on renewing and recrafting their Vision for the business. They realized that in many ways they had a large fruit-stand type of business instead of having a true economic factory. As they considered this situation, they realized they were working *in* their business much more than working *on* their business. This lead them to change their daily roles to focus on overseeing and managing their various areas of responsibility compared to previously when they were doing much of the actual work. These and other changes enabled Sun and the other owners to take their business where they wanted it to go.

ʑʑ

CHAPTER TEN

In Conclusion

There you have it—how to create a thriving business in seven easy steps, how to take your business from where it is to where you want it to go.

As you move forward with your business, by all means refer to this book to refresh your memory regarding these life-changing concepts that will enable you to create a phenomenally thriving and successful business.

So how do you create a thriving business in seven easy steps?

- Step #1—Define a compelling Vision for your business
- Step #2—Identify your business's Critical Success Factors and Strategy
- Step #3—Create a comprehensive Marketing System
- Step #4—Develop an effective Sales Process
- Step #5—Establish a Strategic Advantage via producing your product
- Step #6—Finance your business properly
- Step #7—Apply Innovation and Systematization to your business

If *Creating a Thriving Business* has enabled you to move towards having a thriving business, please do let other current and potential business owners know that there is a book available that is ideal for showing them how to take a business from where it is, to where they want it to go. They will thank you.

ʑʑ

WORKBOOK

An additional resource that will assist you on your journey toward success is the companion step-by-step workbook to this book. Available electronically at *www.FountainheadConsultingGroup.com*, and found under *Resources*, *Products* and then *Workbooks*, the workbook contains many detailed exercises that will assist you in creating an incredibly successful business.

ʑʑ

Now go forth and create the thriving business that you desire!

ABOUT THE AUTHOR

 George Horrigan is Founder and CEO of Fountainhead Consulting Group, Inc. and from his over 25 years of experience being a business planner and a CPA, he has a proven track record of showing people how to start, grow, manage and take their businesses where they want it to go. In fact, over the past 17 years George has shown over 1,200 people either how to grow an existing business or start a new business.

Besides being a noted business planning expert and recognized thought leader, he personally has started and operated seven businesses and understands the mindset and mentality of an entrepreneur, thus giving him both professional and personal perspectives on creating a thriving business. He holds a BA in Accounting and a Masters degree in Financial Information Systems. He is an author, speaker, frequent broadcast media guest, and has been recognized in a number of Who's Who National Registries.

George lives in Atlanta, Georgia.

You can read more at
www.FountainheadConsultingGroup.com

FREE SPECIAL BONUSES

To assist you in *Creating a Thriving Business* Fountainhead Consulting Group, Inc. is providing you with $900 worth of FREE software tools that will speed you on your way to achieving the hopes and dreams for your business.

This special bonus includes a:

- Downloadable CPA-developed, comprehensive Chart of Accounts
- Complete MS Excel® Budget Worksheet
- Fully functioning Break-Even Analysis

To claim your free bonuses just visit
www.FountainheadConsultingGroup.com
and go to Resources, Products and then Book Bonuses
and enter "thriving" to access your free bonuses.

ADDITIONAL RESOURCES

Additional resources are available at
www.FountainheadConsultingGroup.com
that will assist you in *Creating a Thriving Business.*

Printed in the USA
CPSIA information can be obtained
at www.ICGtesting.com
JSHW012049140824
68134JS00035B/3343